HOW TO STEAL FIRE

HOW
TO

 libraries

This book is due for return on or before the last date shown below. It may be renewed by telephone, personal application, fax or post, quoting this date, author, title and the book number.

Glasgow Life and its service brands, including Glasgow Libraries, (found at www.glasgowlife.org.uk) are operating names for Culture and Sport Glasgow.

Glasgow
CITY COUNCIL

How to Steal Fire is the second book on which Stephen and Roger have collaborated. The first, *Life's a Pitch*, was published by Bantam Press in 2007 and went on to become an international bestseller.

HOW TO STEAL FIRE

The myths of creativity exposed,
the truths of creativity explained

Stephen Bayley & Roger Mavity

BANTAM PRESS

LONDON · NEW YORK · TORONTO · SYDNEY · AUCKLAND

TRANSWORLD PUBLISHERS
61–63 Uxbridge Road, London W5 5SA
www.penguin.co.uk

Transworld is part of the Penguin Random House group of companies
whose addresses can be found at global.penguinrandomhouse.com

First published in Great Britain in 2019 by Bantam Press
an imprint of Transworld Publishers

A CIP catalogue record for this book
is available from the British Library.

ISBN 9780593080085

Typeset in 10.5/18pt Malabar LT Pro & 11.75/18pt Neue Haas Unica W1G
by Jouve (UK), Milton Keynes
Printed in China

Penguin Random House is committed to a sustainable
future for our business, our readers and our planet. This book
is made from Forest Stewardship Council® certified paper.

1 3 5 7 9 10 8 6 4 2

'Better to disintegrate than rot.'

This book is dedicated to the self-unemployed.

The minstrel Leonard Cohen saw a connection between error and benefit:

There is a crack in everything
That's how the light gets in.

('Anthem', 1992)

The novelist Howard Jacobson explained:

Savour that! At a stroke, weakness becomes strength and fault becomes virtue. I feel as though original sin has just been re-explained to me. There was no fall. We were born flawed. Flawed is how we were designed to be. Which means we don't need redeeming after all. Light? Why go searching for light? The light already shines from us. It got in through our failings.

Contents

The Book of Revelation

Mad, bad & fascinating to know: inside the creative mind

There is no ending: creativity doesn't recognise boundaries

One point,

two views

About this book

Stupidity has been defined as repeating behaviour and expecting a different result. Indeed, Stephen Bayley and Roger Mavity have done this before: an earlier collaboration was *Life's a Pitch*, but it became a global bestseller, so they have risked trying again. Like that book, this one has two voices. They say the same thing, but try not to repeat themselves.

Roger Mavity's career has been mostly in and around advertising, an environment with ample opportunities to test the hard, bright flame of creativity against the lumpen, drab, grey stuff of harsh and extinguishing reality. He writes with a wisdom that is sometimes rueful but always practical. Once lit, the flame never goes out.

Stephen Bayley is a recovering academic. An early career in universities left him with a didactic streak a mile wide (and, critics say, an inch deep). Later, he became the person for whom 'design guru' was coined. He writes to prompt and suggest, not to explain or justify.

They like to think they make a good double act.

Bayley and Mavity met many years ago in a business world designed by their patron, Terence Conran. In those days, 'Conran' was an eponym for all things creative. Today, Bayley – having midwifed the birth of Conran's Design Museum – is an author, columnist and critic. Mavity – having managed Conran's design and restaurant businesses – is a writer and photographer with an international reputation.

Each of them has written a series of short chapters, identified by their initials and by a different typeface. In keeping with their personalities, Stephen's typeface is traditionally elegant, while Roger's is plainer and blunter. Some chapters debunk the conventional wisdom and fashionable nonsense which surround this arcane subject; others explore the underlying truths.

Creativity includes the whole of God's and man's endeavours, including volcanoes and pop rivets, waterfalls and popcorn, giraffes and Negroni sbagliato, so it's a big subject for a book of conventional size and length. Even to ponder a comprehensive treatment would be an absurd folly. So the chapters are not arranged in a logical narrative sequence, but more as a terrazzo of ideas.

The aim is not authoritative analysis of an ineffable subject, but rather to hint about how to steal fire . . . and ignite thought.

Introduction: a guide for the oppressed

A personal note from one of the authors

Given my own generous endowment of cussedness, lack of realism, demented optimism, pig-headedness, astonishing lack of empathy, reluctance to compromise, tragic lack of patience or humility, inclination to fantasy, toxic vanity and absolute refusal to cooperate on any matter whatsoever, I'm well disposed to sympathise with that legendary figure: The Creative Personality.

Often I champion him and have a stump speech where I talk about the primacy of ideas over admin. Of this I have no doubt. No one cares who was the fixed-cost accountant on the Great Pyramid, but we'd all like to know the bedroom habits of the architect. Or put it this way: the name Ettore Bugatti moves the spirit along more positive vectors than the name Arthur Andersen. No one, surely, needs persuading about creativity.

Ideas are what move civilisation along, giving it point, style and meaning. Creative types have lots. Not because it is good for business, simply

Ideas are what move civilisation along, giving it point, style and meaning. Creative types have lots. Not because it is good for business, simply because it is in their nature.

because it is in their nature. Contrariness is part of the job description. When a government official once asked me how best to stimulate creativity, I said, 'Make it illegal.' Criminalising possession and generation of ideas would stimulate even more than the jug of hock and soda-water that Byron recommended to poets.

The most superlatively creative type I have ever met was the late, great Paul Arden, who, if any single person can make such a claim, established the critical reputation of Saatchi & Saatchi in its Augustan period. I really liked Paul and we became quite close. We went to each other's houses and knew each other's children. Our wives became friends.

I just mention this to put into context what follows. Paul was maddeningly exasperating and contrary. SB (charmingly): 'Isn't it a lovely day?' PA (crossly): 'What do you mean?' We had a project to found a business together. Each of us thought this interesting, but third-party advice was unanimous. They said: 'You must be out of your minds!' We were. That was the point.

Arden and I would never have got anything done, but we would have thought many thoughts. We would have been a Fukushima of high-power futility. So sometimes I wonder if creativity is over-rated, a question discussed briefly later in the book. A lot of people have shapeless, glowing talent, but very few have crisply delineated skill. The workmanlike craft of execution may be just as important to the act of genius as the whack-job creative concept.

The workmanlike craft of execution may be just as important to the act of genius as the whack-job creative concept.

The advertising business was once a fine incubator, or tolerator, of creativity. In this jungle, the creatives roamed freely. And their eccentricities were

6

tolerated because very often those predictably unpredictable eccentricities made the business sing.

But the sun has set on adland. A combination of fragmented media and consumer fatigue means splashy high-spend advertising is no more. And people have got enough stuff. The big challenge today is to be light and free, not to buy a new fridge. As John Ruskin said, 'every increased possession loads us with new weariness'.

So it's difficult for ads to achieve excellence in a culture where people are bored with buying, where great product narratives are a snooze. Factor in advertising's dinosaur–asteroid relationship with new media where the greatest innovation is that what was called 'popular' is now called 'viral' and you'll agree that the Golden Age of Creativity ended when Paul Arden left Saatchi in 1992. At least so far as advertising was concerned.

But this book is not about advertising. Faced with the tepid greyness and timorous conventionality of most decision-making in most organisations, the case for creative behaviour (which sometimes even includes creative *thinking*) is always worth making. But people do not make it very often. So here it is.

Setting fire to thought

How to steal fire

'No single human being can possibly know enough to produce a comprehensive study of all that can be comprised under the heading creativity.'

Anthony Storr, *The Dynamics of Creation* (1972)

[Storr was the respected Cambridge psychiatrist who persuaded Elaine Rosenbloom not to abort the foetus that became Will Self, giving the future novelist a highly nuanced view on creativity. Witheringly, Self said Storr kept a 'colour-coded spice-rack' in his kitchen . . . a remark intended to suggest a certain formulaic dullness in the psychiatrist's thinking.]

▶ *How to Steal Fire* **is a guide for the oppressed. Which is to say, people who are bored by everyday tedium and dismayed by mediocrity. People who reject routine. People like Marcel Duchamp, who regularly contradicted himself so as to avoid conforming to his own taste. People who think: If everyone is different, I want to be the same. It's a manifesto for those who want to zig when others zag. Or perhaps, as the Obamas did, go high when others go low.**

It is an imaginative book about creativity. How could a book on creativity be anything other than imaginative?

But it's not about how to write a symphony or knit an exciting jumper, it's about individuals reclaiming themselves from the anonymous dreariness of a data-driven, collectivised, faceless culture.

It's a human compulsion to be creative, to do and make new things. Without it, we'd still be mired in Proterozoic slime.

It's a human compulsion to be creative, to do and make new things. Without it, we'd still be mired in Proterozoic slime.

Maurice Saatchi once said that creativity is the last legal way of getting an unfair advantage in business. But if creativity is legal, it is not always moral or ethical. In a signature act of creativity, Prometheus *stole* fire from the gods. Theft is often involved in creativity. Hence, the title.

Creative people are entirely comfortable with theft (sometimes called inspiration, plagiarism or misappropriation). Picasso said: 'Great artists don't borrow, they steal.' Although some people attribute this epigram to T. S. Eliot. Perhaps they stole it from each other, which rather proves the point. Anyway, 'steal like an artist' is one way to avoid oppression.

And creative people do not bother to indulge their audiences, being more inclined to please themselves. David Bowie said: 'All my big mistakes are when I try to second-guess or please an audience. My work is always stronger when I get very self-ish about it.'

Creativity boosters often tell us to 'think outside the box', but that's a cliché, which is itself a denial of the creative spirit, which always tends towards the original, the unusual and the contrary. To the creative, there *is* no box. There are no conventions of any sort in creativity.

And that's about the only conventional aspect of it. Creativity is a most uncertain matter. Einstein said: 'If I knew what I was doing, it wouldn't be research.' Miles Davis, when asked what he was going to play, replied: 'I'll play it first and tell you what it is afterwards.' Picasso was against common sense. Whoever would want *common* sense? Karl Lagerfeld says that clear thinking, employed inopportunely, stifles creativity. Some people would call this ragbag of attitudinising difficult and cussed. Others would call it creative. But the results are there for everyone to admire.

The simple truth is: we do not know where ideas come from. Clearly, what we call creativity involves large-scale pattern-recognition, our

> There are no conventions of any sort in creativity. And that's about the only conventional aspect of it.

brains crunching huge data sets and improvising a result. Some people can simply see wider and deeper than others, finding more diverse sources of inspiration and arranging them in novel ways to impressive and influential effect. Designers, especially, seem to see the world in a different way.

Steve Jobs, founder of Apple, said, 'Creativity is just connecting things,' although he perhaps intuited it was rather more as well. He was also very good at connecting and collecting, or, as some would say, stealing. In Jobs's case, connecting a GPS-enabled cellular phone with a touchscreen to the internet to create the smartphone. Both the cellular network and GPS, as well as the internet, existed before the iPhone of 2007, but Jobs's creative connection changed the world

Setting fire to thought

forever. He saw something no one else had seen. It might yet prove to be the single most influential (which is not necessarily to say 'beneficial') creative act ever. At least, since Genesis.

But then, of course, you also need the power of execution. It's no use, as they used to say in the eighteenth century, to be in possession of imaginative genius if you lack the technical skills to express your vision. Jobs was, incidentally, fortunate to own a successful computer manufacturer. Without that, he would have remained an eccentric visionary, a loopy Californian airhead with bad manners and unsatisfactory personal hygiene.

Philosophers and neurosurgeons are agreed that they do not really have a clue how, at the Steve Jobs level, the brain works. But artists are often more matter-of-fact: Leonardo looked at damp stains to get inspiration; Brahms said music came to him without the exercise of conscious thought. Meanwhile, Jobs did Zen and macrobiotics.

The painter Stanley Spencer on the other hand, or rather on both knees, found sniffing lavatory bowls a reliable stimulus to his art. A famous car designer is inspired by looking at trainers. Hard exercise, danger and long holidays can also be stimulating. So too can drink and drugs. The majority of US Nobel Laureates in Literature have been hopeless drunks.

But no one has ever found a reliable method of generating ideas, although people do keep trying. There is still a tendency in business to suggest that groupthink is the way to do it. This horrible intellectual collectivism has been accelerated in the past generation by the increasing influence of fast, but essentially dumb, electronic networks in our crowded and over-busy lives.

The world population has doubled since the fifties. Over fifty years ago Intel founder Gordon Moore declared a 'Law' that chip memory doubled about every eighteen months, during that time when the population has, thanks to Jobs and others, had ever easier access to ever more clever devices. It now seems likely that, surprisingly soon, anybody who wants one will have a smartphone. Jerusalem! Actually, no.

This ecstasy of connectivity has encouraged some excitable people to say that we have left the era of autonomous individual creativity as surely as we have left the era of child sacrifice, public executions, ducking witches, monochrome television and free parking in city centres.

But the digital world is a terrible disappointment. Nothing is less cool than data. The internet has undermined newspapers, magazines and books; it has devalued research and put us all under pitiless surveillance. All this in exchange for the opportunity to send pictures of skateboarding hamsters instantaneously around the world.

James Surowiecki's influential book *The Wisdom of Crowds* (2004) argued for an amazing creative democracy where the responsibility of developing ideas is devolved to the consumer, not to the creative genius. Never mind that this has not actually happened. Never mind that if it did, the results would be melancholy: would you prefer that the check-out queue planned your dinner or would you prefer to have a gently perspiring and finger-lickin' Nigella Lawson over a hot six-burner? This form of groupthink may be wrong and rather dated, but it remains, nonetheless, persuasive.

Besides, no one is going to bed tonight dreaming about digital encryption. *How to Steal Fire* suggests an approach to life where you don't have to be a passive supplicant to data, but instead become an active participant in a more rewarding personal activity. Namely, thinking.

One of the great deceptions, ruinous fallacies and lazy excuses in contemporary life, and especially in contemporary business life, is the belief that 'teams' get things done. In his great book *The School of Genius* (1988), the psychiatrist Anthony Storr argued convincingly that being alone with your own thoughts is the most reliable and productive method of generating ideas. There's a continuing debate here, but it's an important opinion.

The focus group is one example. Herein, politicians or manufacturers of edible fats, too timid to launch a campaign or a product with heroic conviction, secure the approval of a room of bored housewives who have been paid twenty-five pounds, tube fare and some yoghurt tokens to turn up and offer faked opinions. It is not difficult to see what poor quality ideas, with denominators lower than the Puerto Rico Trench – lower than whale shit, to use Frank Sinatra's impressive expression – emerge from focus groups.

Then there is 'brainstorming', an invention of the Mad Men era on Madison Avenue. The concept of brainstorming was, paradoxically, an autonomous creative act by an individual called Alex Osborn, one of the founders of the BBDO ad agency. In his book *Applied Imagination* (1953), Osborn showed how groups of people, sometimes a mix of experts and novices, might perhaps generate new ideas. But group dynamics, subtle pressures and a reluctance to be truly outspoken usually combine to mean that brainstorming produces, at best, a light, irritating drizzle of complacent mediocrity.

So far from being liberating and democratic, brainstorming sessions are just evidence of the strange tendency towards Soviet-style collectivism and thought-management in American life. Anyone who has been to Atlanta's Varsity restaurant, the world's largest, will have sensed that this was what the Electricians' Union refectory in Magnitogorsk might have been like in 1928.

It is exactly the same with PowerPoint. This is not really an efficient and invigorating presentation tool. Quite the opposite: PowerPoint encourages dull, linear thinking and disguises platitudinous structures by neat graphics. Brainstorms and PowerPoint are the democracy of a Parliament of Fools. Creative people have no use for them. Wiki is for lazy dullards.

So, instead of production-line thinking, consider instead our romantic ideas of great artists, or even great scientists, at work. Schubert in his garret; Picasso harassing a canvas in his studio at Vallauris; Newton in his Cambridge exile; Elon Musk in his Jacuzzi.

Great thoughts come to inspired individuals, not to weary groups. The great poet of solitude was Henry David Thoreau, who decided to live alone in the Massachusetts woods. He wrote: 'I had three chairs in my house; one for solitude, two for friendship, three for society.' In solitary exhilaration, Thoreau wrote one of the great inspirational books: *Walden* was published in 1854 and has been a counter-culture classic ever since.

> **Great thoughts come to inspired individuals, not to weary groups.**

From here it is a short step to Steve Jobs chewing mung beans on his Kyoto moon-viewing platform. (Although it is worth noting that Thoreau's conception of solitariness was something of a grandiose creative delusion – or a deception: his solitary hut was on the outskirts of a bustling little town and, essentially, at the bottom of his mum's garden.)

But as every Zen adept knows, whatever is true, the opposite is truer. For every argument in favour of solitary genius being the source of creativity, there is an equal and opposite argument in favour of the group. This is why artists so often founded colonies to share ideas. Certainly, the Bauhaus cannot be compared to an away-day with brainstorming about germ-management run by a chemical company in Princes Risborough, but it was nonetheless an expression of collective will.

How to Steal Fire does not have to answer to asked or unasked questions because this is not a textbook of any sort, and certainly not a technical study of psychological states. Instead, it is designed as a brain-prompt. Possibly an irritant. Although you could start at the beginning and work towards the end, that would be a pedestrian sort of progress. *How to Steal Fire* is not even intended to be read sequentially. Why would you want to do that?

But who are the oppressed, for whom this book is a guide? Anybody who works in a stultifying environment where people go to meetings, use flipcharts, mangle jargon and talk in brainless clichés. And anybody who runs their life as an assault on stupid bureaucracy and dull authority will find here their first draft of a future manifesto. *How to Steal Fire* says: Let's do it! No matter what anybody else says.

Does creativity even matter?

We talk a lot about creativity. Large corporations hold seminars on how they can become more creative. In ad agencies, the 'creatives' are treated with awe, as if they were gifted with special powers – the witch doctors of modern marketing. Innovation is worshipped, no longer just as a means to an end, but almost as an end in itself.

The very word 'creativity' is becoming so over-used that it is in danger of losing its real meaning. It's a bit like the word 'designer', which used to mean something significant: namely a person who designed things. But with excessive and unthinking use it has now come to be merely a shorthand for anything with pretensions to be a little better than average: as in 'designer handbag', which really just means 'over-priced handbag'. One of the more irritating examples of this current devaluation of language occurs when newly built houses are described as 'architect-designed'. Who else would design a house – your doctor, or the local butcher perhaps?

So is the concept of creativity going down the same slippery slope, simply becoming another meaningless cliché?

I think not. Creativity is not some activity, like skating or yoga, which might go in or out of fashion. On the contrary, creativity is as essential to our lives together as a pulse is to our bodies. Mankind's creative curiosity about what might be possible has led to any number of discoveries and inventions.

Somewhere, some time in the past, someone noticed that when a round object rolled, it was much easier to move – and the wheel was invented. All kinds of food and drink owe their existence to creative curiosity. Wondering about grapes, and their juice, eventually gave us wine. Somewhere, at some time, someone must have experimented with crushing grain, and discovered flour. Then they experimented with what you might do with this new invention and, lo and behold, mankind had bread to eat. The invention of the alphabet, without which any written communication is not possible, was a truly creative moment. And now we find it hard to imagine life without the internet and a smartphone. It's not just modern ideas that matter: the Stone Age was the period when man invented the idea of making tools, initially from stone. Thus, civilisation was born.

> **Creativity is not some activity, like skating or yoga, which might go in or out of fashion. On the contrary, creativity is as essential to our lives together as a pulse is to our bodies.**

It's not all good, of course. Experimenting curiously with what happens if you roll up the leaf of a tobacco plant and set fire to the end has given us cigarettes, and consequently has also given us epidemic levels of lung cancer. Creative curiosity about what happens if an atom – in theory an indivisible unit – is divided has given us a valuable new energy source; and it has also given us the nuclear bomb, Hiroshima and Nagasaki, and a fragile world order.

Creative curiosity can lead us down some dangerous paths. But, for all that, it is our creativity that has separated humanity from the beasts.

So, creativity matters. Which makes it worth understanding how it operates, how it can be understood, and how it can be inspired.

Prometheus, Shiva & creation myths

▶ **Creativity is prehistoric. The very first thing that ever happened was creative. The booming, resonant, terrible voice of Genesis says: 'In the beginning God created the heaven and the earth.' And, of course, He did this *ex nihilo*. There was nothing before, no precedents, no models, no exemplars, no prototypes. He did not even have a brief. We struggle to comprehend this and that's exactly how it should be: if creativity was easy to understand, anyone could be creative.**

The strangeness remains. How it happened is a mystery impenetrable to earthlings, but this Christian idea of the Creation had a practical and lasting effect on our imaginations.

The Bible has given us a conviction that there is a beginning and an end to all things and that, in between, there is valuable forward progress to be made. If you believe in the End of the World, you acquire a special dynamic of thought. You put things behind you. You move on. You see things in front of you. By contrast, Tao cosmology does not recognise a single moment of creation (because, Taoists say, there always was something). Meanwhile, Hindu cosmology does not share the Christian idea of progress, which the cycle of creation–existence–annihilation so powerfully suggests. Hindus have a less determined sense of beginnings and ends.

So, here we are with a blank piece of paper – and, at the moment, a blank mind – the genesis of a book. Or, more accurately, thirty or so virgin B5 Muji notebooks corresponding to all of the following (presently unwritten) chapters. My reaction to this prospect of blank and vacuous horror? I simply believe an idea or two will be along in a minute. No one knows where ideas come from, but they do arrive. The End of the Book may not be as calamitous as the End of the World, and certainly more easy to predict with accuracy, but readers can decide in umpteen pages' time whether this creative swagger is justified.

Creation and Destruction are mysteriously linked. 'The major advances in civilization', mathematician Alfred North Whitehead believed, 'are processes that all but wreck the society in which they occur.' Many questions are to be begged there. But the creation–destruction link is well rehearsed. The anarchist Bakunin said, '*Die Lust der Zerstörung ist zugleich eine Schaffende Lust!*', which more or less means the desire to destroy is also the desire to create. And so it is.

There is no more disturbing evidence of this than the events of 16 July 1945 at Alamogordo in the Chihuahua Desert of New Mexico. Here was the detonation of the first nuclear bomb. Its creator was J. Robert Oppenheimer, leader of the Manhattan Project. The awful result, witnesses said, was like a thousand simultaneous suns. Oppenheimer simply noted of the atrocious explosion: 'It worked,' and added, 'A few people laughed, a few people cried, most were silent.'

On 6 and 9 August that year, the people of Hiroshima and Nagasaki discovered precisely how well this genre of weapons worked. In 1965 NBC made a memorable television documentary, *The Decision to Drop the Bomb*. In it you can see Oppenheimer, one of the greatest nuclear physicists of his day and a party to the decision, reciting in incantatory style a part of verse 32 of Chapter II of the *Bhagavadgita*: 'Now I am become Death, the destroyer of worlds.' His voice is trembling, perhaps a little histrionically. The reference is to Shiva, the Hindu god for whom destruction and creation are mixed. Terrible and beautiful, simultaneously. Two years later, Oppenheimer was dead.

All cultures have 'creation myths'. Soon we may need destruction myths as well. While Christians believe the will of a paternalistic God was the original creative act, other religions believe the cracking of cosmic eggs for a sort of mundane omelette gave rise to our world. This cosmic egg theory, of course, is not yet unproven. Among Native Americans, there are tribes who believe the world arose from divine breath. It would be small-minded to deny the possibility. The truth may be somewhere between eggs and breath.

The Incas of South America had their god Viracocha rising from Lake Titicaca in frightful darkness and creating beneficent light, a process greatly facilitated by his wearing, as their art shows, the sun as a crown and holding dramatic lightning bolts in each hand. What's common to all creation myths is a sense that, whether describing the Christian God at the primeval abyss or the First Nations tribes with wind or water and God's breath, all present a sacred history describing our escape from an earlier state of evil chaos.

But the myth that has the most relevance to modern creativity is Prometheus. He was a trickster and a Titan, a second-division Greek god. The circumstances are muddled, as they often are in Greek mythology, but Prometheus had been demoted by Zeus on account of a trick he had played. By way of revenge, Prometheus made a visit to Mount Olympus and mischievously stole fire from its guardians, Hephaistos and Athena, with a view to passing it on to mortals. (The fire-stealing motif appears in non-Western mythologies too.) And here is the big metaphor: the gift of fire empowered man to build and create.

Fire put man at the level of the gods themselves, as creativity so often does. With fire you could make bricks and cast iron for ploughshares. With fire you could eventually build nuclear weapons, drive cars and eat at McDonald's. Fire made civilisation possible. But we acquired fire by an act of theft. It's almost a version of original sin.

> **Fire put man at the level of the gods themselves, as creativity so often does.**

In some etymologies the name Prometheus might mean 'having foresight', but our Prometheus did not anticipate his fate. For this treachery, he was punished for all eternity by being chained to a rock and having, daily, his liver nibbled by an eagle. To the ancient Greeks, the liver had a symbolism similar to our heart: it was where emotions are seated. The meaning is clear: when humans become creative, they imitate or even usurp the gods. And they will suffer for their efforts.

But a minor and more dilute version of the creation myth is often employed by artists, writers and designers anxious to establish unique credentials. Ernest Hemingway, of whom rather more elsewhere, was an outstanding example. He created a personal mythology of the writer as man of action, a performer of brave and heroic deeds, not a scholarly and wimpish recluse. So persuasive did this all become that, aged sixty-one, Hemingway found himself quite incapable of matching the reality to the mythology and, depressed and confused, looked out his Scott pigeon gun, loaded it and shot himself one lonely afternoon in Idaho.

Perhaps inspired fantasy, even outrageous lies, were involved in Hemingway's personal creation mythology. But so too was great art. Talking about *The Sun Also Rises* (1926), a scriptural source of Hemingway lore, what with all its drinking and its bullfighting, his friend Scott Fitzgerald, of whom we will also read more elsewhere, said, 'The fact that it may be "true" is utterly immaterial.' Instead,

Fitzgerald recognised and applauded the superiority (the preferability) of the 'imagined to the seen, not to say the merely recounted'.

Thus, theft and fantasy are both elements of creativity; perhaps their presence is even a test for it. But there are sterner definitions of it too. '*Numero pondere et mensura Deus omnia condidit*' was the antiquarian William Stukeley's account of Newton's analysis of the Creation: the physicist said, 'God created everything by number, weight and measure.'

That's a mechanical view of things. And we can argue with it. What's certain is that stealing fire is always a very deliberate act, if not always a measurable one.

What does 'creative' really mean?

We use the word 'creative' often, but are we truly clear what we mean when we say it? Frequently it's an adjective that's applied to artistic events, like a ballet or an exhibition of paintings. That's fine as far as it goes, but if we assume creativity is only to do with the arts, I think we're rather missing the point. Of course, a ballet can be creative; though it doesn't have to be, and sadly I've been to a few that definitely weren't. But creativity lives in a much wider world: creativity can exist in virtually every aspect of the human experience.

Talk to a parent of small children about how kids deal with their shoes before they're at an age when they've mastered the shoelace knot. You'll quickly realise that the invention of Velcro was transformational for tiny kids getting their shoes on and off. (How did we cope before Velcro came along? No, I can't remember either.) So, the invention of Velcro was indeed a creative act.

One of Britain's aristocrats in the eighteenth century was so addicted to gambling that he wouldn't leave the gaming tables, even to eat. Consequently, he invented the idea of putting a slice of meat between two slices of bread so he could eat and gamble at the same time: surely a fine creative act. The fourth Earl of Sandwich gave his name to his invention, and the sandwich remains a staple of our diet two hundred years later.

Think about driving on a motorway. It's a much, much quicker type of road than any other. What makes a motorway different? Answer: it's the only road that has no junctions, no roundabouts, no turns to right or left: you can only enter or leave by a slip road to the slow lane. This incredibly simple concept has transformed long journeys. Yet it involves no new equipment, no new technology: it simply takes what is there already and uses it in a different way. The result is not only much faster journey times: paradoxically, motorways are much safer per mile driven than ordinary roads. So I would regard the invention of the motorway as a genuinely creative act.

Putting on a play by Shakespeare may be an artistic act, but that does not mean it's necessarily creative. But the first time Shakespeare was performed in modern dress was a highly creative moment, because it forced people to reassess the great writer's work: it gave a new perspective on an old and well-established piece. It helps, of course, that Shakespeare's themes are so timeless. That's what makes a modern-dress version so valid – it underlines the play's contemporary relevance.

> **Putting on a play by Shakespeare may be an artistic act, but that does not mean it's necessarily creative.**

You can find creativity in business too. Once, when I was running a design company, we were trying to sign a deal with a big Japanese corporation. But there was a stumbling block. We wanted a clause in the contract that said that, if one side sued the other, the case would be contested under English law. Unsurprisingly, the Japanese wanted a clause saying that any litigation would be under Japanese law. Neither side would budge, and a deal which both sides wanted was in real danger of collapse.

Then I came up with a possible answer. I suggested that if the Japanese wanted to take us to court, they would have to do so under

English law; and if we English wanted to take them to court, we would have to do so under Japanese law. Of course, neither side would want to litigate under another country's law, so you could say my proposal was preposterous – but it was equally preposterous for both sides. Moreover, the difficulty of litigating in an alien culture was a great disincentive to litigation in the first place. The outcome was that the contract was signed, and both sides were happy. Immodestly, I'd describe my answer as creative, in that it solved a tricky problem in an original way.

What then are we learning about creativity? First, that it's a talent which can be applied to any aspect of life. Second, that it necessarily involves an element of innovation: anything which is an echo of what is already there cannot be truly creative.

In creativity, as these examples suggest, there is often also an element of problem-solving. But there doesn't have to be: take a look at the painting opposite, *The Anger of the Gods*, by the Belgian surrealist René Magritte:

This strange picture may be provocative, but it certainly doesn't solve any problems. Indeed, it offers us questions rather than answers. Yet it would, I believe, be described as 'creative' by most of us.

Why? Because, I suggest, it shows an imagined world beyond the real world we know and recognise. It takes us to a different place, one which is slightly comic yet at the same time unsettling, even threatening.

The two main elements within the painting are quite familiar: a businessman is being driven in his limousine; and a jockey is galloping on his racehorse. There's nothing unusual about either of those things, notwithstanding the fact that the car is quaintly ancient. The picture was painted in 1960, just one year before the launch of the famously svelte E-Type Jaguar, so Magritte's choice of car and passenger deliberately recalls an earlier era, but there is still nothing

The Anger of the Gods, René Magritte

inherently weird about them. Similarly, the horse and rider look no different from what you might see at any race meeting at Newmarket or Sandown Park. So the ingredients are familiar. What is utterly unfamiliar – and the key to the painting's mesmeric effect – is the juxtaposition of the objects. We see jockeys riding racehorses and we see chauffeur-driven cars. But we don't generally see one on top of the other.

The juxtaposition of the car and the jockey is made more bizarre by the fact that the car is being driven with an apparent steady calm, while the jockey is driving his horse in a frenzied gallop to the unseen winning post.

We've seen how creativity can, in the case of Velcro or the motorway, offer clearly discernible and practical advantages over what was available before. In that sense, both concepts are innovative.

Magritte's painting is also innovative, in the sense that before Magritte there was no one painting like him. But, unlike Velcro or motorways, it offers us no practical benefit: instead it offers us stimulation, intrigue, something which makes us think and wonder.

So the uses of creativity may be pragmatic or they may be cerebral, even spiritual. But underlying the notion of creativity is the concept that it must be innovative: it must show us an aspect of the world in a new and different way.

For that innovation to happen, the person responsible for the creative concept must have made a connection between ideas which had not been made before. Every creative thought depends on such a leap of the imagination.

But a leap of the imagination is spontaneous, by definition something impossible to plan or arrange in an orderly way. We can recognise it when it's happened, but we don't know how to make it happen. Therein lies the fascination, the almost unsolvable intrigue of creativity.

Why are books on creativity so dull?

▶ **The answer is: many are written by people who do not know (or care) what they are talking about. There is a large literature on creativity, most of it dispiriting.**

Here's a really terrible sentence – ill considered, over-long, lumpy and effortful – from Darrin M. McMahon's *Divine Fury: A History of Genius* (2013): 'Students of ancient mythology and religion have taken pains to show that this general temporal orientation was common to the wisdom traditions and great world religions that took shape in the so-called Axial age that spanned the first millennium BCE.'

There is either too much or not enough here. Certainly, not enough genius. Of tropes, clichés and redundancies, there is much to be said. Professor McMahon (for I imagine him to be of professorial rank) has not thought ahead. Nor has he employed fantasy or theft. Nor discipline. Nor has he seen a new way to express an existing idea. 'What oft was thought, but ne'er so well expressed' as Pope defined wit. And we suffer for it. He needs some theft. But if you are going to thieve well, you need targets and aspirations.

Writing well is perhaps a discipline worth acquiring for those intent on stealing fire, since it reveals a mind that is alert. There are no rules, but there are useful pointers. In *The Reader Over Your Shoulder* (1943), the poet Robert Graves advised that, when you have written something, you cross out all the bits you are most pleased with. Perhaps Professor McMahon, had he followed this advice, would have nothing at all left. Or what about Detroit crime writer Elmore Leonard, who encouraged careful revision of texts, counselling: if it reads like writing, rewrite it? These are other examples of the creative mentality and its taste for destruction.

Good writing is based on a judicious balance between careful planning and inspired spontaneity. There should also be a little theft involved too, since great writers are always happy to sit on the shoulders of their giant predecessors, as I have so often done here. Every word should count. Double-check for repetitions or redundancies. While the rules of grammar are, for the creative, there to be ignored, best to check for careless agreements and metaphorical inconsistencies. Sounds, for example, do not 'reflect' things but 'echo' them. A tragedy is not at all the same as a calamity, despite what BBC News insists. Pedantry is a refuge of the scoundrel, but it keeps you sharp. Always ask if there is a smarter, shorter or newer way to express an idea. Always.

David Bohm's *On Creativity* (1996) has become something of a standard work, although it is such a dull and unconvincing book that it's more a deterrent than a stimulus. Look at this unhappy thing and think: If this is 'creativity', then we surely want nothing to do with it. Bohm was interested in theoretical physics, neuropsychology and the philosophy of mind. Alas, his interests did not extend to literary style or graphic design.

Although he was born in Wilkes-Barre, Pennsylvania, and died in London, the Anglophone Bohm writes English as if it were not his first language. More likely, second or third. Nor has he learnt the art of precis. And he enjoys a space- and time-wasting trope. Empty-headed formulae including 'As was indicated in the previous section' appear everywhere. If you had indicated it properly in the first place, there would be no need to employ such literary flatus. It is unnecessary and spoils the reader's neurones.

Then there is the design of Bohm's book *On Creativity*. Clearly, neither author nor publisher saw any conceptual or practical connection between the stated objectives of the book and the book itself. It is quite stunningly, insultingly un-designed: the white-out-of-grey back cover blurb is illegible without magnification. The body of the text is set on the page so artlessly that it runs into the gutters. And where it does not, it slops heavily around like a turgid grey ocean of tired words.

A good book, especially a good book on creativity, of all things, should have image and text conceived as one. A superlative example of this, and an inspiration here, was Quentin Fiore's redesign of Marshall McLuhan's *The Medium is the Massage*, co-ordinated by Jerome Agel in 1967. It is a book of startling visual juxtapositions and expressive typography. Unforgettable to anyone who has ever seen it.

The title is a play on the famous phrase – 'the medium is the message' – that first appeared in McLuhan's *Understanding Media* three years before. McLuhan enjoyed the interplay between 'message', 'Mass Age' and 'massage' and, while it was said to be a printer's error, he was, being creative, happy to go along with the messaging mistake. The result is an immortal book.

Scientists do not, perhaps, see metaphors as readily as artists or writers do. Nor do they like accidents quite so much, preferring the illusory sanctuary of numbers and the groupthink of peer evaluation. But as A. N. Whitehead warned: 'Insistence on clarity at all costs is based on sheer superstition as to the mode in which human intelligence functions. Our reasonings grasp at straws for premises and float on gossamers for deductions.' Sometimes numbers lie.

The scientists' refusal to make connections between thought and action is the more sad because the technical world of measurable things is a treasury of stimulus. Take, for example, Nikolaus Otto's description of the four-stroke cycle in the petrol engine he defined. Induction, Compression, Ignition, Exhaust can be expressed as Suck, Squeeze, Bang, Blow. And that's nearly poetry.

Or consider robots, for so long the darlings of voyeuristic technological thought. A robotic arm is said to have six degrees of freedom and with these you can precisely describe the exact position of it in space. First there are yaw, pitch and roll. Second there are surge (forwards–backwards), heave (up–down) and sway (left–right). That is beautiful: every position defined, The Universe plotted in six words.

Suck, squeeze, bang, blow, yaw, pitch, roll, surge, heave and sway – I find these words curiously inspiring. Sometimes I recite them. Each could be a chapter in a book. If there were more explosions and strange connections in books about creativity, they would be so much more interesting. No more 'general temporal orientations' or 'as was indicated in the previous section'. Maybe this sounds nagging and intolerant, but this is just the way creative people think.

The fear of the unfamiliar

Creativity is nothing if not problematic. It seems ferociously difficult to know how to inspire it. Every creator has experienced some kind of writer's block, or artist's block, or plain idea generator's block. Most great artists and writers have suffered bouts of emotional despair when the idea just won't come. At a more mundane level, even the simplest act of imagination, like choosing a birthday present for a friend, can be alarmingly perplexing. All too often, the act of trying to think of an idea simply produces a kind of constipation of the brain.

And when the idea eventually appears, it seems worryingly difficult to know how to judge it. That's not just an individual problem; it afflicts us collectively too. When we all share one clear opinion, history usually proves us wrong. The night that Pirandello first staged *Six Characters in Search of an Author*, he was roundly booed by his Roman audience. It is now recognised as one of the most important dramas of the twentieth century. Stravinsky's *Rite of Spring*, today seen as a seminal work of classical music, was greeted with derisive laughter followed by general uproar when it was first performed.

When Manet completed his masterpiece *Le Déjeuner sur l'herbe*, it was so reviled that he was forbidden to exhibit it in the show for which it had been painted, and he had to invent his own 'Salon des Refusés' ('The Rejects Show' in plain English) to get it in front of the

Le Déjeuner sur l'herbe, Edouard Manet. A reject yesterday, a masterpiece today

public. It is now recognised as one of the truly great paintings of the nineteenth century.

In more recent times, J. K. Rowling's first Harry Potter book was rejected by no fewer than twelve publishers. (You don't need me to tell you what happened when the thirteenth publisher said yes.) And Robert Pirsig's extraordinary book of philosophical enquiry, *Zen and the Art of Motorcycle Maintenance*, was allegedly turned down by over a hundred publishers. It has since sold more than five million copies.

The list goes on.

Why is it that we can't spot 'good' when it jumps up and punches us in the face?

The truth is that we probably can recognise, and cope with, 'good'. The problems start when we get to 'very good' or, even worse, 'exceptional'. Anything which is exceptional must, by definition, be highly unusual, and therefore different from what we're used to. And because it's different from what we're used to, we can't explain it, categorise it, deal with it. Humans are, as a species, uncomfortable with the unfamiliar. We find it threatening.

That is why creativity is such a vexing subject. Our instinctive fear of the unfamiliar means that our first response to anything exceptional will be to treat it, unconsciously, as an attack on what we know and trust. We may eventually come round to seeing its merit, but it will be a slow process.

It's a conundrum and a contradiction: we know that innovation is necessary and desirable. Obviously we cannot repeat the same ideas for-

Our instinctive fear of the unfamiliar means that our first response to anything exceptional will be to treat it, unconsciously, as an attack on what we know and trust.

ever. We know we need new thinking. But 'new' equals 'unfamiliar' and we are threatened by the unfamiliar. So we want new, but when we get it, we don't like it.

It's complicated by the fact that 'new' and 'good' are not necessarily the same. Sometimes, the reverse is true. So when we see avant-garde art, we know that we're supposed to be open-minded and like it. But we also know the fable of the Emperor's new clothes, and we see echoes of that in the modern art world. How do we tell, when we look at the art of today, who is a talent and who is a charlatan?

The truth, disappointingly perhaps, is that we can't tell immediately. There are two reasons for this.

First, it takes time for the world to be able to judge what is good and what is meretricious. Cream rises to the top, and dregs sink to the bottom, but both processes are gradual. We have to live with new ideas for quite a while before we can really make a considered judgement about them.

Second, the art world has always suffered from a corrosive relationship with money. Artists may be interested in art, but art dealers are more interested in their next Ferrari, or that house in the Hamptons. And dealers are powerful people: without them, the artist will never get his work to the public. So art is frequently presented as more remarkable and significant than it actually is, because the art dealer stands to gain from that.

Your definition of a great work of art might be something that moves you deeply, but a dealer's definition of a great work is simply something he can sell. Small wonder that the art of today is presented to us with an exaggerated notion of its worth. An art dealer's gift is to give you, the potential buyer, confidence in something you feel nervous about.

An art dealer understands that we all want to embrace the new but, when we are confronted by it, our innate fear of the unfamiliar gets in the way.

Homo sapiens is a species with strong reluctance to appreciate new ideas, to welcome anything into our lives that does not already have a place there. This is one of the great stumbling blocks to producing, or

'Without deviation from the norm, progress is not possible.'

enjoying, original creative ideas; and it's a reluctance we need to fight against.

Frank Zappa summed it up perfectly when he said, 'Without deviation from the norm, progress is not possible.'

Quantifying creativity: would you like to borrow my template?

Can you quantify creativity? Surely, anything small enough to be measured is trivial? You might as well try to calibrate love, fear, wit or hope. Or weigh sunshine.

But is there a formula, a proven method, to aid creativity? If there was a reliable one, creativity might not, perhaps, be so rare. Here we enter the dismal swamps of abstruse conjecture.

Historically, there is ample evidence that effort plays a part, although how big a one is very uncertain. Michelangelo insisted that if people knew how hard he had struggled to gain his mastery, they would lose their sense of wonder. The Laurentian Library was the obvious bonus from an earlier investment. His effort was as admirable as his results and the former made the latter possible, he argued. Bach said something similar. To which we probably say phooey.

This puritanical notion of effort's relationship to reward took recent form in Malcolm Gladwell's *Outliers* (2008). Here he argued that ten thousand hours of practice were what you needed as a basis of excellence. The idea was soon refuted by people who argued that this was all very well in disciplines such as classical music or chess, where the rules were well established, but the ten-thousand-hour notion applied less certainly to creativity, where the rules are not, and never will be, written. Doing ten thousand hours of exactly what would have made *Sgt Pepper* possible?

In any case, K. Anders Ericsson, whose 1993 paper 'The Role of Deliberate Practice in the Acquisition of Expert Performance' was the source of *Outliers*, said Gladwell had crudely simplified the original academic argument. Gladwell replied that he never said ten thousand hours was enough: to be great, you needed genius as well.

Neuroscientists cannot convincingly explain creativity, although some of them continue to try. There is lots of brain space, they say, between input and output and here is where creativity occurs with synapses popping unpredictably and fruitfully. There's plenty of room in the cerebellum to get usefully lost on the neural pathways. Additionally, Darwinians believe we have an evolutionary need for novelty, for the next-new-thing. These, then, are the conditions for creativity: a mixture of motive and opportunity.

What do artists have to say? Sir Joshua Reynolds founded London's Royal Academy on the belief that rules are an inspiration to genius, not an impediment to it. Meanwhile, his contemporary Mozart's compositional method depended on eclectic borrowings and established formulae. But architects of genius use the same bricks as jerry-builders.

Robert Frost believed that rules helped poetry. Free verse, he said, was like playing tennis without a net; a beautiful image. Agatha Christie used a template: her most popular novels have almost identical structures and characterisation. Paul and John explained that once they had written the first verse of a Beatles song, then everything else followed. So with this evidence, we are somewhere between disciplined structure and intuitive mysticism.

There has been an obstinate notion among progressive educationalists that creativity can be taught. As an educational equivalent to the easy listening of Mid-century Modern, a view began to emerge, especially among American psychologists, that creativity was not restricted to Mozart and Michelangelo, but was a part of every individual's potential, just as an Eames chair might one day be a part of everyone's dream home.

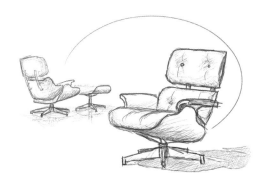

Richard Buckminster Fuller always used to say that everyone is born a creative genius, yet the struggle of existence de-geniuses most of us. But the come-to-Jesus-everyone's-creative movement was always bedevilled by vague abstractions in place of hard data or what T. A. Razik none too beautifully called 'concrete referents'. The thing about creativity is that concrete referents do not exist, a truth that technicians entombed in viewless evidence-based boxes cannot see.

Absurdly, traditional educational methods to encourage creativity often emphasise 'convergent thinking' because it is safer and more predictable. Targets are known, behaviours can be imitated, results can be achieved! Except they rarely are. Creative types are more likely to ignore (or possibly fake) evidence. And fake (or ignore) results. You cannot even describe the creative mentality as 'divergent thinking', because that, while offering more scope for exciting variation than the convergent sort, is still restrictive. Divergent from what? they ask.

In 1965 the psychologist E. P. Torrance even brought 'design' into consideration, although this was more than a decade after Ulm's Hochschule für Gestaltung had begun to teach 'systematic design', a very German and very pedagogic belief that there was a single, correct way to design, say, a tape-recorder and that a strict method might be followed so as to arrive at ideal results. In that the great designer Dieter Rams was one of its products, Ulm's 'systematic design' can be said to have achieved some sort of lasting success.

Torrance developed a 'Product Improvement Test', inviting children to enhance their toys through useful play, an idea which (probably unconsciously) imitated the Bauhaus's learning-by-doing methodology. Torrance also proposed tests called 'Ask and guess' and 'Just suppose'.

Meanwhile, at the University of California's Institute for Personality Assessment, researchers were still sifting the data from Donald MacKinnon's 1962 study of American architects. The research found that there was no simple correlation between IQ and creativity. On the contrary, the most creative individuals were rarely straight-A students, although that is not to say that assessment is itself a reliable indicator of anything other than the assessment process. (And this applied to research scientists as well as building designers, most of whom were solid B graders.) The most talented architects in this study would not make it into graduate school. Thus, formal education was found to be deliberately excluding creative individuals. And if procedures could not exclude them, then teaching methods would be sure to inhibit whatever weak current of creativity survived. But this much we know.

One of the most recent reappearances of the creative teaching chimaera is SIT, the acronym of Systematic Inventive Thinking, a method developed at Tel Aviv University in the nineties. Derived from Russian megadata of an ever so slightly totalitarian and sinister character, SIT proposes that the process of invention can be analysed, understood and repeated.

This is odd, because the bulk of the observational evidence is that creativity tends to flourish when in opposition to formal systems of any sort. Genius is raw, not refined. At this moment, SIT (which is taught in Wharton Business School and other leading establishments) has invented nothing of note.

Presumably, creativity is not systematic at all. If it can be measured, calibrated or quantified, it cannot be very interesting.

I am,

therefore

I think

Where *do* ideas come from?

▶ This is, of course, the huge and seemingly unanswerable question of creativity. Do ideas come from debate with others, from silent deliberation, from thorough research?

No, they don't. The answer to the big question of where ideas come from is rather surprising – ideas come from an area immediately above your kidneys. That's where your adrenal glands are situated, and these glands are the organ that creates adrenalin, the chemical that arouses us to urgent response. In the USA, adrenalin is more commonly called 'epinephrine', a term coined by the American biologist John Abel, which derives from the Greek for 'above the kidneys'.

If a human faces a sudden threat or challenge, those glands above the kidneys go into action. They produce a flood of adrenalin which stimulates whatever part of the body is needed to cope with the threat: so if you have to flee from a masked intruder in your house, those muscles which are used in running will be stimulated to enable you to run faster than you've ever run before. If you have to defend yourself from attack, your body will be much stronger than it normally is because it's being supported by a sudden dose of adrenalin.

But threats aren't only physical. If you're a writer, there is the threat that you won't get the money your publisher has promised you if you don't meet the deadline you've agreed with him. So as the deadline looms, those glands above your kidneys start to work overtime. Adrenalin is produced, your mind is stimulated, and magically the ideas start to flow.

I used to work with David Abbott, one of advertising's great creative talents, who founded Abbott Mead Vickers, which went on to become London's largest and most admired advertising agency. David's surface demeanour was one of astonishing calm and control. But when he needed to produce an advertising campaign, he became a master of procrastination. On one occasion, we had three weeks to produce ideas for a new campaign. After three weeks minus one day, David had nothing to show. The presentation was booked for 9 a.m. the following day. I asked David how it was going. 'Nothing yet,' he said. 'You'll just have to be a bit patient. I've got other stuff today, but I'll do it at home tonight.'

The next morning, I came in half an hour before the meeting and waited anxiously. With ten minutes to go, I heard David's car come into the car park. He stepped into the office with a sheaf of drawings under his arm.

He spread them out in front of me, and they were brilliant.

'My God,' I said, 'you had a productive evening last night.'

'Not really,' he replied. 'I couldn't get any decent ideas last night, so I went to bed, got up at five this morning, and then the ideas flowed.'

David's sangfroid under pressure was impressive. But I never knew whether his apparent calm was an act to reassure me or to reassure himself.

Some creators avoid putting pen to paper, or paint to canvas, until the very last minute: they know that the imminent deadline, hurtling towards them like a train in a tunnel, is the only lever to get that adrenalin flowing. Having worked in advertising for many years, the 'leave it to the last minute, then the idea will come' syndrome is one with which I'm depressingly familiar.

But others have followed the opposite logic, and worked with obsessively exaggerated self-discipline to stimulate the adrenalin flow. The stress of awaiting the deadline is replaced by the stress of forcing oneself to perform. Novelist and playwright W. Somerset Maugham wrote from breakfast to noon every day of his life, Christmas Day included. This was regardless of whether he had anything to say. He then stopped for the rest of the day, even if he was in full flow. But this apparently severe discipline masked a huge unease about his ability to deliver. He famously said, 'There are three rules for writing a novel. Unfortunately, no one knows what they are.'

> **'There are three rules for writing a novel. Unfortunately, no one knows what they are.'**

We like to think that creativity, being a positive force, derives from positive circumstances: an environment of warmth and tranquillity. But usually the reverse is true. What gets creativity going is stress. That may be the kind of stress we've been talking about, such as an imminent deadline. But there are other kinds of stress. Poverty is a good example, and the cliché of the artist starving in a garret has real truth. An empty stomach is a powerful incentive to produce a painting that will capture someone's imagination.

Possibly the most potent form of stress for an artist is not the pressure that comes from without, but the pressure that comes from within: namely some internal emotional turbulence.

If you study the lives of great painters, writers, composers, you find a continuing theme: they all too often suffer some kind of extreme inner turmoil. Van Gogh's huge depression, which led to him taking his own life at the tragically early age of thirty-seven, is perhaps the most famous example. But there are many others. Beethoven's life was blighted by having an alcoholic father, by the death of his mother when he was still a teenager, the death of his brother at the age of forty-one, plus his own continuing ill health and intensifying deafness. Yet out of this pain came the desire, the need even, to produce some of the greatest music the world has ever heard.

Suicides among creative people are common. In recent times, Diane Arbus, the brilliant but controversial photographer, suffered greatly from depression, and took an overdose of barbiturates and cut her wrists at the age of forty-eight. Mark Rothko, the celebrated painter, also suffered from depression and took his own life when he was sixty-six. The English writer Virginia Woolf drowned herself at the age of fifty-nine. The American writer Sylvia Plath neatly sealed the door of her kitchen with tape and towels to protect her children in the next room, and then put her head in the gas oven at the age of thirty.

The list goes on and on. This only serves to demonstrate that the creative mind and the depressive mind are inexorably interwoven. Artists – meaning not just painters but musicians, writers, sculptors, film makers and more – don't do what they do because they want to: they do it because they have to. Their creativity is how they purge themselves of the pain they feel inside.

This may seem a gloomy take on the creative condition, but it's a fair one nonetheless. Creativity is bound up with innovation, and the desire to do things in a better way or to express feelings with a new intensity. That in turn is bound up with dissatisfaction. No inventor ever tried to find a better way of doing something unless they were dissatisfied with the present methods. No writer ever proselytised for a better world if they thought the existing world was fine, thank you very much. Creativity is a currency, like all coins, with two sides. On one side is the excitement of the new idea, but on the other side we see huge discontent with the status quo. It is just that discontent which acts as the spur to creativity.

If you want a creative idea, don't ask a happy man: it is discontent with how things are today that inspires the mind to seek a better route for tomorrow.

Montaigne: happiness is an incentive to mediocrity

This is something of a crass paraphrase of Michel Eyquem de Montaigne's higher thinking, but happy people can't be arsed to do anything. On the other hand, creative people always want to change things. Why would you jeopardise happiness through change? *Si ce n'est pas cassé, ne le répare pas*, **as Montaigne himself might have said. If it ain't broke, don't fix it.**

And if you believe that, it may also be true that anguish, in all its hellish varieties, is a stimulus to creativity. 'Hence, vain deluding joys' is the first line of Milton's 'Il Penseroso'. Joy is not productive, the poet says. But the ill humour black bile is. From the Greek words for black bile comes our word 'melancholy'. And since Aristotle, black bile is the humour associated with creativity.

Why are creative people often so melancholy? Because the nature of their insights allows them to see disturbing problems as well as exciting opportunities.

But a word first about mediocrity. It is a disposition towards the mean, an avoidance of extremes either high or low, good or bad, happy or sad. Mediocrity results from lazy habits of mind, from living in the past and from being fearful of the future. Mediocrity does not, perhaps, fully engage in the multitude of opportunities always afforded by the present moment. The mediocre state of mind has a taste for cliché and no talent for précis. She is incapable of visualisation and sluggish in making connections or seeking diversions.

It needs to be admitted that misfortunes, especially including childhood trauma and adult anxiety, can be powerful influencers of the creative spirit. Felicity in childhood is demonstrably not always a benefit. Stress can be our friend. Many creative people thrive on fear and insecurity, seeking out difficulties.

To some psychologists, creativity can be understood only as a morbid state, a remedy for a flawed world. Michelangelo could only find real peace when wandering alone around the woods near Spoleto. Puccini believed 'art is disease'. It was that painful. The novelist W. G. Sebald encouraged contemplation of our 'dismal plight' because it might stimulate stratagems to avoid it. In one novel he has a paragraph nine pages long. Perhaps he was thinking this when he crashed his Peugeot and died on a Norfolk country road.

Many creative people thrive on fear and insecurity, seeking out difficulties.

Montaigne's *Essays* (1580, English translation 1603) are among the wisest and most civilised conversations in the literary canon. He wrote them at leisure and luxury in the tower of his chateau in Guyenne in the Dordogne whither he retired from public to consider the delights, mysteries and absurdities of existence. These he then wrote about with unusual wit and wisdom.

The tower was raised above a chapel with a vaulted ceiling. His bedroom was above and, on idle days, he could hear Mass without getting out of bed. Above the bedroom was a library and a study, which

Montaigne had decorated with classical nudes and maxims from Lucretius, Horace and the Bible. The learned graffiti included one in French: 'A sa liberté, à sa tranquillité et à son loisir'.

But what of happiness? It is so elusive and rare that you might even question its existence. But then, it is thought, when you say you do not believe in unicorns, a unicorn dies. Perhaps, as Alberto Moravia believed, we are at our happiest when we do not realise it. Meaning that happiness is not cartwheeling naked down the street, whooping with joy, but that state of calm contentment that is satisfying, not stimulating.

That was Montaigne's reading as he languished in delicious comfort with his library of books and his jugs of Bordeaux. Never mind that in his own state of calm and perhaps slightly tipsy contentment, Montaigne managed to arse himself to write one of Europe's great works of literature, running to over a thousand pages in a recent edition, but if you wish to steal fire there may be an argument for getting cross, or a case to be made for making yourself uncomfortable.

Using evidence-based analytical tools, emotional or physical stress appears to be highly productive. Just read Tchaikovsky's letters. Depressive people are clinically unhappy. However, a roll-call of the great depressives would include Newton, Baudelaire, Dickens, Churchill, Proust, Evelyn Waugh, Graham Greene and Kurt Cobain. 'Grief', Proust believed, 'develops the powers of the mind.' Clearly, artistically speaking, there is much to be said for depression, unhappiness and grief.

So what are our stratagems for creating a condition of productive misery? Starving yourself might be an idea, but it won't quite do. The sinister Minnesota Starvation Experiment of 1945 showed that its subjects soon became irritable and socially withdrawn (thus mimicking a caricature of the creative personality), but also, less positively, that they found concentration difficult and experienced harrowing lapses in judgement.

However, stopping short of systematic starvation, a mild, nagging hunger may be a reliable stimulus to action since, when you are hungry, powerful, evolutionary survival responses become alert. But possibly the most stimulating condition of misery is penury. Escaping the gravitational pull of poverty was, for example, the making of Henry Ford.

Richard Layard is the author of *The Annual Happiness Report* and *Happiness: Lessons from a New Science* (2005). The ambition of this LSE economist was no less than to alter the parameters of classical economics, insisting that happiness and not income was the true measure of economic success. Companies, Layard said, should audit the well-being of the workforce and include the figures along with the P & L in their annual reports. Of course, this is an engaging idea, as both Tony Blair and David Cameron found, even if there was no effective methodology for evaluating well-being: happiness tends to be mute and dumb, while misery is reliably articulate.

FORD MOTOR CARS

Illustrating Four Posi tions of the Model T Touring Car with Top

Serviceable and of very pleasing appearance from every view point

WATCH THE FORDS GO BY

That's a beguiling paradox in human affairs, but if Henry Ford had been happy with the mind-numbing tedium of life on a Midwest farm, he would never have created the gasoline buggy.

The price of paint

┈┈┈┈┈┈┈┈┈┈┈┈┈┈┈┈┈┈▶ **There's a saying that when art critics meet, they talk about the philosophy of art, but when artists meet, they talk about the price of paint.**

It's a joke which makes a significant point. Looking at the world of creativity from the outside, it can seem an arena of high ideals, deep thought and wide vision. But looked at from the inside, it's much more pragmatic territory. Artists don't just need a great idea, they also need to pay the rent, buy dinner, find somewhere to publish their work, and keep themselves sane when the muse is on holiday.

One of the great American musical composers was asked which came first, the lyrics or the tunes. His reply was blunt: 'The contract comes first.' Creatives have to deal with practicalities as well as dreams.

This point is well demonstrated in architecture. We admire the beautiful columns of the Parthenon, and we compare Ionic, Doric and Corinthian styles of column when looking at classical architecture. But these great pillars were not designed to look beautiful, they were designed to stop the roof falling down. Of course, the architect also wanted to achieve beauty, but that was, ultimately, a bonus.

Stunning modern buildings, like Mies van der Rohe's magnificent Seagram Building in New York, owe much of their grace to the brilliance of the architect. But they are also indebted to the invention of curtain walling, whereby the building is supported by an inner core, allowing materials like glass to be used for the outer walls.

Practical inventions don't only influence creativity in architecture. The Italian Renaissance produced some of the greatest art the Western world has seen. Part of that is due to the genius of men like da Vinci and Michelangelo. But part was due to the invention of oil paint, which replaced egg tempera, and gave artists the chance to create images with a luminosity and brilliance which hadn't been possible before.

And we should remember, while dwelling on practicalities, the influence of hard cash. The astonishing flowering of creativity in the Renaissance was in part due to the incredible wealth of the city states, like Florence and Venice; not forgetting the desire of the rich families who ran them, particularly the Borgias and the Medici, to flaunt that wealth. A great artist needs a great patron.

The marriage between inspiration and hard practicality is something we can see exemplified more recently, in Victorian Britain. The bridges of Brunel and magnificent railway stations like Paddington and St Pancras combined an aesthetic of high Victorian flamboyance with the ability to perform a very demanding practical task. These buildings were the cathedrals of the new religion of industrialisation. Like the cathedrals of earlier times, they had to perform functionally as buildings, but they also had to perform inspirationally as art.

In earlier times, creativity was seen to be an important spur to both scientific and artistic thinking: da Vinci was an imaginative engineer as well as a brilliant painter, and another chapter in this book explores the creativity behind Isaac Newton's theory of gravitation. But now a rift has developed: at school age we are forced to choose between science and arts subjects, as if they were two utterly different ways of thinking. This seems to me to be dangerous.

It pigeonholes scientists as types who may be cerebral but can't be imaginative. Yet Darwin's *On the Origin of Species* (1859) was a gigantic imaginative leap. Observing the different species on the Galapagos Islands, where Darwin made his breakthrough, was a purely analytical task: but understanding how and why those species evolved the way they did was a groundbreaking creative step.

Equally, divorcing the arts from the sciences tends to dismiss artistic endeavour as something which may be thought-provoking but is, nonetheless, essentially peripheral. It's as if you're allowed to be practical or you're allowed to be imaginative, but it's a sin to be both. Nothing could be further from the real truth: as those highly creative artists, grumbling about the price of paint, will tell you.

When the problem becomes the solution

Conceptual artist Cara Mills was struggling to find an idea for the installation that was to be the centrepiece of her new show. She produced dozens of ideas, none of them good enough. They all, she felt, deserved to be shredded.

And that gloomy thought, she suddenly realised, was to be her inspiration. She printed all her ideas on a long roll of paper, connected the roll to a shredder mounted on the ceiling, and switched on. As the rejected ideas were shredded, the paper fragments gradually formed a picturesque white mountain. Her installation had become a striking metaphor for the creative struggle – as you can see from the image on the next page.

Cara is not the only person to have discovered that the creative solution is best found by immersing yourself in the problem.

I had a similar insight with John McConnell, one of Europe's leading graphic designers. He explained to me the importance of the initial briefing from the client, and said that he would interrogate the client at length about every aspect and every detail of his problem. He confided in me that the ideas for some of his best work actually came to him in that first briefing stage. The more thorough that first exploration of the problem, the more likely it was that the solution

The Labour of Ideas, Cara Mills

would flash into John's mind before he had even left the client's office to go back to his studio.

'Of course,' he added cheekily, 'I never told them that. I'd make them wait two or three weeks before showing them the answer. If they knew how quickly I'd got to a solution, they wouldn't have thought it worth paying for.'

You may think John's remark was said tongue in cheek, but knowing John well, I doubt that. He had identified one of the great truths of creativity: namely, the real value of creative talent is utterly different from the perceived value. John knows that the value of his idea lies in the idea itself, not in how long it took him to conceive. But the customers of creativity, like a business buying an advertising campaign or an individual buying a painting, tend to judge value by the trappings of the idea – how long it took, how hard it was to execute – not the intrinsic worth of the idea itself. One celebrated art collector would measure any painting he was contemplating buying, then divide the area by the cost to calculate the price per square foot. It's easy to ridicule this until you realise that major art dealers, other things being equal, charge more for a large work than a small one.

And there is the old cliché of the man looking at an abstract and saying, 'My child of five could have done that.' The writer and artist Susie Hodge has written a whole book specifically to refute this notion. But a simpler way might be to give your five-year-old a canvas and some paints and see how many lifetimes you have to wait before a masterpiece appears.

People who lack instinctive creative insight search for some objective measure of worth – how long it took to complete, how big it is, how difficult it was to execute. People with creative insight know that none of that matters: the only question is, how good is it?

In John McConnell's example, the real point is that the client was paying for John's innate talent and his experience, not how long it took to come up with the idea. But John was savvy enough to know that a client might not see it that way.

John's insight was to understand that if he immersed himself utterly in the problem, the solution would almost grow of its own accord. Cara Mills, with her wonderful 'bad-idea shredding machine', discovered the same truth.

Ultimately the only criterion that counts is simply, 'Is it a good solution?' But as we have seen, the best route to that good solution is not always to pursue it as an end in itself, but to wallow in the problem and allow the solution to emerge in its own good time.

Get lost! Or, Can cities be too stimulating?

▶ **When Tom Wolfe's epochal anti-hero, Sherman McCoy, nervously took the wrong off-ramp in a dark part of New York, he got lost in the badlands. And the misadventure created shocking, life-changing, accidental trouble, giving rise to the chief motif in the landmark novel of the late twentieth century: 1987's *Bonfire of the Vanities*.**

Getting lost produces delicious fear. It undermines certainty; it challenges self-identity. And these are good things. Granted, had McCoy's Mercedes-Benz been fitted with GPS, Wolfe's story would never have begun. GPS has leached a lot of healthy fear and mystery from life. Now, getting lost may be a thing of the past. But in the matter of being helpful to creativity, getting lost is at least as interesting as staying at home. Why? Because getting lost introduces you to new places . . . and to new people, as Sherman McCoy discovered.

Mozart often worked at home, played billiards and had a pet starling who could sing his piano concertos if things became dull. Italy's second greatest poet after Dante was Giacomo Leopardi. He led a solitary, short existence. Although his work made him famous throughout Europe, he preferred to live alone. He is an absolute paradigm of the idea that great creative minds are not impaired, but possibly enhanced, by isolation. Iris Origo explains this in her superb biography *Leopardi: A Study in Solitude* (1974).

But is creativity best left to itself, a billiard table, a singing starling, a lonely cell and a writing desk? Or might there be other conditions to encourage it? Despite the protestations about a digital wired culture allowing creativity to flourish in isolation, the unbending fact remains that most creative activity still, even with high-speed internet, occurs in dense, crowded, old-fashioned cities.

Or in vast campuses such as the one Norman Foster has just designed for Apple. Just why do all these Californian techies need to be together and attend group zero-gravity aerial yoga sessions? The tumult of old Huangzhou during the Han Dynasty, what Eric Wiener described in *The Geography of Genius* (2016) as 'constant pandemonium', gave rise to wood-block printing and the first sex manual: *The Biography of Emperor Wu*.

A theory called the Strength of Weak Ties supports this. Namely, it is more stimulating to know a lot of people a little than to be constrained by firm commitments to close family and a tight-knit group of friends. Apple's Steve Jobs, according to his biographer Walter Isaacson, believed that creativity arises from chance encounters and random discussions and spontaneous whatnot. Things that make you say 'wow'. Jobs was, of course, adroit at stealing. He could not have built Apple as a desert anchorite. He had to be in the Bay Area, not Death Valley.

San Jose is the centre of what's now called Silicon Valley. It was once regarded as the boonies. In Burt Bacharach's famous song 'Do you know the way to San Jose?' the bathetic idea is: if you couldn't make it in LA, you needed to beat it back to the Bay Area. But a swelling of interesting people and opportunities has now made the area around San Jose the most prosperous place on earth.

Places that inspire creativity do not have to be pleasant. Belgravia is spacious, safe, clean, secure, expensive and opulent, and every house is serviced by docile servants and most have passenger lifts.

The park is a short limo ride away. Yet Belgravia is dead and unproductive. There is no Belgravia School of anything at all. Meanwhile, Liverpool is decayed, melancholy, turbulent, grubby and romantic. Liverpool, by contrast, has produced a disproportionate number of artists, writers and musicians. Thieves too. If you want to steal fire, Merseyside rather than Eaton Square would be a good place to start.

And you do not find creativity in the countryside. Peace, calm and fresh air maybe, but creativity, no. Cities are the source of all animation, and street life animates cities. Great streets are frontiers; and a frontier is not a topographic mark on a map, but a state of mind. The dirtier and more dangerous the street, the more likely it is to be inspiring.

Seen from outer space, or even just from the earthbound Castel San Elmo, Spaccanapoli is a two-kilometre wound that separates the chaotic city of Naples. It is a survival of the old Roman *decumanus inferiore*, the southernmost of the main streets that formed the grid pattern of the Graeco-Roman city of Neapolis. It means 'Naples-splitter', but it is not truly divisive. On the contrary, Spaccanapoli is an axis of creativity.

Along Spaccanapoli you will find vials of the blood of San Gennaro, *friggitorie* selling deep-fried pizza – fast food was invented here – hookers, old maids fearing *malocchio*, demented baroque churches and the Palazzo Marigliano. The wound gives clarity to chaos.

Naples may have a reputation for crime, dirt and disorder, but every successful city needs its Spaccanapoli. London's Soho is comparable: it became a creative centre because low rents encouraged small businesses, and a tradition of acceptance beginning with Huguenot immigrants of the seventeenth century encouraged a tolerance of artists. When Soho was sordid, it was creative. You do not find artists or interesting businesses in Belgravia.

So to encourage creativity, build a Spaccanapoli wherever you can: a spectacular street with drama, comedy, chaos, beauty, pizza, hookers, smells, the evil eye and occasional sightings of God. You can build this in your imagination.

Opinion seems entirely split about whether small or large communities do a better job of encouraging creativity. Hans-Ulrich Gombrecht of Stanford University believes that small communities are better. But Benjamin Barber has argued in *If Mayors Ruled the World* (2013) that the optimal organisation unit for humans is a large urban agglomeration.

But what sorts of cities encourage civilised activity? It is worth remembering that Athens was at its peak for only a single generation. And what might have contributed to Athens's extraordinary creative vitality was that it was, like Liverpool, isolated from everything else. And, if not isolated, it was confrontational: as Nietzsche remarked, the superlative Athens of Pericles was challenged on every front. Moreover, in Athens the agora encouraged citizens to walk about. Walking about is more cerebrally stimulating than sitting down.

To be creative, cities probably have to be quite nasty. That Florence is situated in a disablingly humid, malarial valley where summer storms of epic ferocity interrupt everyday life did not hinder the Renaissance. Instead, Wiener says in *The Geography of Genius*, 'Florence was . . . an "empire of things" to borrow a phrase from Henry James.' Here Leonardo Fibonacci adopted Arabic numerals and precise mathematical calculation became possible because the old Roman numerals had never allowed such a thing. The Florentines gave us modern currency in the florin. Banking started here. Today in foetid Mumbai nothing works very well, so people are forced to improvise, innovate and develop highly creative avoidance strategies. So Mumbai daily enriches itself.

Big cities are good places to get lost in. Mumbai would be an example. If you get lost, you will rapidly develop survival strategies. But GPS has made getting lost impossible. And therefore more desirable.

Turn the GPS off.

Boredom & ennui

Let's get the weary joke out of the way immediately. Boredom is very interesting. Possibly creatively stimulating. And becoming more so by the day. 'Boredom' is a recent coinage, but so too is 'creativity'. Of course boredom and creativity are related.

Ripples of excitement are animating the still, sluggish waters of academe. A new discipline (actually) called Boredom Studies is emerging. We have a New Boredom. So, far from being a negative state of mind larded with miserable streaks of lethargy, apathy, self-loathing, hopelessness and misery, there's a growing body of opinion, both artistic and scientific, that boredom may be, or can be considered as, a positive stimulus to creativity and to enterprise.

Writers with block know the distressing symptoms of the Old Boredom: a feeling of uselessness with a nasty sense of being unable to escape the condition. You are trapped in a bad place where there is no hope of immediate improvement and no prospect of future relief: it's a Hades of futility whence there is no release. A limbo where tastes are dulled and appetites atrophied. Boredom is, according to Tolstoy, 'the desire for desires', of craving something we find difficult to identify. But Boredom, in the new reading, may be good for you.

Henry Ford is a fine example. Boredom inspired Ford's tinkering mechanical genius and gave us the Model-T, motorising the world and expanding the hitherto narrow horizons of, first, Midwest farmers, then, next, all the rest of us. To a degree, that's what car users still feel today: that they are escaping life on the farm. Ignoring all rational, practical and moral arguments against the use of motor vehicles, individuals choose to drive because it promises a release from a boredom that's resident at home. Wherever home might be. Even your humble Ford Fiesta comes fully accessorised with vistas of escape.

'Driving is boring, but it's what we do. Most of American life is driving somewhere and then driving back wondering why the hell you went.'

But John Updike, still on nodding terms with the Old Boredom, makes Rabbit say: 'Driving is boring, but it's what we do. Most of American life is driving somewhere and then driving back wondering why the hell you went.' Certainly, for most of us the frustration of traffic daily refreshes the sensation of boredom. The feeling of being hopelessly trapped – as you do in a river of hot, coagulated, fume-spewing metal – is one of the defining conditions of being bored.

But a scientifically credible definition of boredom remains elusive. Wijnand van Tilburg is a researcher who says: 'Because the scientific study of boredom is still in its infancy, we keep finding new and often surprising features of it. The traditional view is that it's a passive, disengaged state. But boredom has an exciting side: it rouses a search for purpose.' The New Boredom is, in van Tilburg's words, pro-social: it is a fruitful field ready to be cultivated.

'Bored to death' is a familiar expression suggesting something complex and frightening about boredom's relationship to extermination. Can we be so bored that the very last flicker of enthusiasm for life expires and we become permanently defunct? Is our repugnance about the Old Boredom simply a fear that apathy and lethargy may inexorably slide into death itself?

Maybe, but then there is the contrary evidence that death-defying, life-threatening activities are a reliable escape from boredom's dull grip. I doubt, for example, that BASE jumpers feel bored when throwing themselves into Norwegian fjords. Anybody looking for excitement, even danger, is engaged in an escape from the threat of boredom. In this sense, boredom is a great motivator.

Being bored, if we are lucky, makes us wistful for lost pleasures or desirous of future prospects of them. Nostalgia, sometimes said to be a psychosis, is a yearning to be somewhere else historically speaking. And it is a symptom of boredom. In this sense, the New Boredom is a deluxe emotion enjoyed in cultures that have risen above subsistence: knuckle-dragging hunter-gatherers were perhaps never bored since the mere struggle for survival consumed all their physical and psychological resources. You are only bored because you can imagine circumstances superior to your own humdrum here and now.

If you are bored, you want to move on. Van Tilburg says: 'Boredom is an emotion that helps us find meaning in life. It feels unpleasant and can cause harm, but it also reconnects people with valuable others from their pasts, makes people more willing to help those in need and strengthens commitment to heroes.' You can argue that boredom is thrilling because your listless, glum, bored individual acknowledges the existence of better worlds . . . if only he could find them. Being bored can be the beginning of a creative journey.

French *ennui* is not quite the same as boredom. This *dégout de la vie*, or distaste for life, has an etymology shared with the word meaning annoying. In teasing out a definition, it's important to distinguish mere irritation (which is a nuisance) from stultifying boredom (which is an all-consuming funk).

At Tate Modern there is a painting by W. R. Sickert called *Ennui*. It shows a deadly brown parlour of about 1914. A husband is slumped at a table, the wife stares at the wall. A bell jar of stuffed birds is a symbol of boredom's entrapment. It is surely an English Sunday afternoon, a condition for which there is still no cure. There is nothing to do and nowhere to go. The couple suffers in the same way Updike's New England swingers suffer at that deadly time of the afternoon when, all passion spent, there is simply nothing else to look forward to.

Vistas and vectors of escape – in space and time – are everywhere in the discussion of boredom. The bored want escape from the prison of now into the freedom of the past or the future. They want escape from stultifying security into life-enhancing risk. Surely only the bored would go surfing? What a remedy that might have been for Sickert's couple.

So what makes us bored? People, certainly; absence of them perhaps less so. Amusingly, thinking of an interminable cocktail party, John Updike said: 'A healthy male adult bore consumes each year one and a half times his own weight in other people's patience.'

And so to the Boredom Threshold: what tips us from the pleasantness of everyday life into the crushing misery of boredom? My own top-of-the-head shortlist, doubtless similar to others, includes: actors, politicians, concerts, airport delays, queuing of any sort (but especially in Post Offices), hold music, VAT, any conversation about the internet, Brexit or children's schools, getting a car serviced, T&Cs, flipcharts, PowerPoint and trains which stop in the middle of nowhere. If I had any experience of knotting carpets, I would add that too. Repetitive tasks are reliably boring.

But real boredom runs deeper.

Writers, the most solitary of creatures, often toy with boredom because it fascinates and disturbs. Oscar Wilde wrote a poem about it: 'Taedium Vitae'. The novelist Alberto Moravia used to walk about Rome and, according to his translator William Weaver, would say to anybody he met: '*Mi annoio. Voglio morire.*' ('I'm bored. I want to die.') Although Moravia was, by most accounts, a humorous and good-natured soul who meant nothing of the sort. He wasn't really bored and didn't want to die.

Moravia's novel *La Noia* was published by Bompiani in 1960. Here, Weaver said, Moravia 'and his old enemy, boredom, came boldly to grips'. Indeed, *La Noia* is the SUV of boredom literature. Moravia writes:

The feeling of boredom originates for me in a sense of the absurdity of a reality which is insufficient, or anyhow unable, to convince me of its own effective existence . . . For me, therefore, boredom is not only the inability to escape from myself but is also the consciousness that theoretically I might be able to disengage myself from it, thanks to a miracle of some sort.

But the question of time passing either too fast or too slow always recurs in the discussion of boredom, and here is the elegiac thing: happy people rush towards death as time whizzes by, while, for the bored, time seems endless. Evelyn Waugh, for example, thought 'punctuality is the virtue of the bored'.

John Cage 'wrote' an extremely boring piece of music called *4'33"*, which refers to the precisely four minutes and thirty-three seconds you listen to the absolute silence that he authored. Cage said: 'If something is boring after two minutes, try it for four. If still boring, try it for eight, sixteen, thirty-two, and so on. Eventually, one discovers it's not boring at all but very interesting.'

Now we are getting somewhere. The New Boredom suggests we can have too much stimulus in our over-busy world. If we have any sense, we might want to cultivate boredom to overcome the noise of so many conflicting signals, the better to concentrate on our real desires. And the occasional creative insight.

I can't get no satisfaction

We all assume that it's good to be happy; and we all assume that it's bad to be complacent. But these two states aren't that far apart. To be happy is to be satisfied with one's lot; and to be complacent is also to be satisfied with one's lot, to the point that our normal self-critical faculty starts to doze off.**

We like the notion of being satisfied, because satisfaction equates to contentment, and that's something we all seek. But isn't the moment that you are satisfied also the moment you stop striving?

People who are highly innovative rarely, if ever, achieve satisfaction. You have to be dissatisfied with something in order to want to improve it, to seek a better way. That's why the creative mind is endlessly restless: it's always trying to solve a problem or do something in a better way – which of course clearly implies that there is a problem to be solved or that the present way isn't good enough.

When Steve Jobs was transforming Apple from a basket case into the largest company in the world, he was, for a while, preoccupied with making mobile phones smaller. His team brought their latest prototype into Jobs's office. They were satisfied: it was much smaller than anything that had been seen before. Jobs was not satisfied: he thought it still wasn't small enough. Without saying a word, he picked up the costly prototype and dropped it into the fish tank which adorned his office. There was a wait; and then a few bubbles emerged and floated to the top. Jobs had made his point – if there was air in the phone, it could be made smaller. Jobs was more creative than his colleagues, not because he had a larger level of imagination but because he had a larger level of dissatisfaction. So he set the bar higher.

It's often assumed, in business management for example, or in the training of people in sport, that it's important to be highly motivated. That's true – but don't think that motivated people are the same as happy people. On the contrary, to be motivated means that you have a hunger to do something which hasn't yet been done. So you're dissatisfied, and you'll only be satisfied when you achieve higher profits, or run in a record time, or beat whatever goal you've set yourself. Except that when you've done that, you still won't be satisfied, because it's not in your nature.

Essential to creativity is a ferocious dissatisfaction with the status quo. The artists of the Renaissance discovered the technique of perspective in painting because they were dissatisfied with the style of painting that prevailed at the time: it wasn't realistic enough. So they had to invent a new style. Four hundred years later, the French impressionists were equally dissatisfied with the painting of the time: it was too realistic. Perfection of portrayal had produced a kind of blandness in emotional communication. They wanted to find a way of going beyond representation to get closer to real feeling.

If you go to Tate Britain and visit the room with all those wonderful Turners, you can observe how this great artist's style changed as he grew older. When you look at the paintings yourself, be sure also to look at the dates: you can trace how Turner himself gets dissatisfied with his own work. As a young man, Turner painted landscapes and seascapes that are both beautiful and realistic. They are fine paintings, but it wouldn't be unkind to say that they are good, but not great. It's clear that Turner felt that too: it's a mark of his genius that he became dissatisfied with his own creations.

So he developed his style, and his pictures become much less realistic, yet much more powerful. The dramatic seascapes of his late years tell us that Turner was no longer interested in showing what it looked like to be in a storm at sea: he wanted to show what it felt like. The pictures tell a tale of man in a state of constant dissatisfaction, a man endlessly searching for a better way.

Here's a painting by Turner from 1810.

Petworth, seat of the Earl of Egremont, William Turner

Contrast that with a much later Turner, painted in 1842.

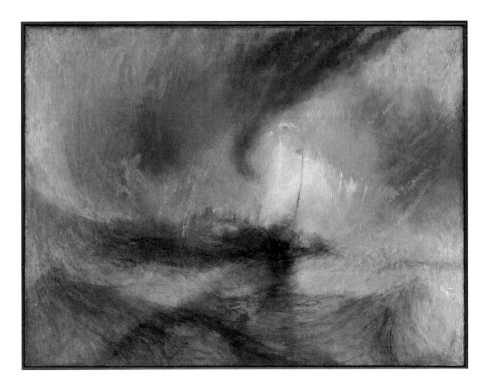

Snow Storm – Steamboat off a Harbour's Mouth, **William Turner**

The earlier painting is gracious enough, and beautifully painted, but it doesn't stir the soul. The later painting is startlingly dramatic and powerful. It's an image that overwhelms the viewer.

As Turner matured, he didn't achieve the contentment we might hope for in our older years. On the contrary, he was fired by a raging dissatisfaction with his own work, a passion to take it to a higher level.

It's just one instance of a fundamental truth: creativity is only achieved by those in a high state of dissatisfaction. The creative mind is never happy with the status quo, but unremittingly restless in the search for a better path.

Sit down &
make yourself
uncomfortable

'E 'l mio riposo son questi disagi.' (**'And my rest is these troubles.'**) **That was Michelangelo describing how he found rest in discomfort. Not only is psychological discomfort, the storied anguish of the great artists, stimulating. Physical discomfort can be useful as well. Alec Issigonis, the designer of the Mini, deliberately made his marvellous little car's driving position uncomfortable so as to keep the driver helpfully alert.**

There is a famous essay in the history of design called 'The Sitting Position – A Question of Method'. The author, Joseph Rykwert, was fascinated by how it is really quite hard to make an absolutely convincing case either way when asked the question: 'Is comfort a distraction?'

He was also interested in our cultural prejudices when it came to sitting: ergonomic studies in the Second World War indicated that the most functional position for a pilot was to lie prone. But that went against centuries of tradition, so fighter and bomber pilots remained sitting in something which absurdly replicated the posture of a drawing-room armchair.

Two of the greatest symbols of American indolence are the BarcaLounger and La-Z-Boy armchairs: Cadillac Eldorados of the furniture universe – over-stuffed, obsolete, vulgar and guiltily magnificent. It's a fair bet that none of America's (mostly tipsy) Nobel

Laureates in Literature ever owned one. They would have been more productive standing on a parapet with pigeon spikes. Certainly, Ernest Hemingway did his writing standing up at a lectern (with a glass of Scotch at hand).

But for every creative man of action, battle-scarred and fatigued, writing at a lectern, there is a creative man of leisure, swamped by velour, central heating, pot pourri and damask drapes. Marcel Proust and Hemingway are the perfect examples here. The indolent Frenchman's life was remarkably uneventful when compared to the American's. He was a man of inaction.

Their prose styles reflect, to put it no more explicitly, different ways of life: Proust's enormous, rambling *In Search of Lost Time* contains several sentences of about a thousand languid words, including very many adjectives and adverbs. Hemingway, by contrast, is reputed to have written a whole short story in a mere six words.

And who was the greater writer? Fire stealers are not necessarily audacious adventurers, they can be mummy's-boy stay-at-homes whose sense of an adventure was a gentle trip to Cabourg, not shooting an elephant or throttling a lion on the veldt.

While Hemingway craved adventure, Proust conducted a life-long search for comfort, which concluded with his occupying a cork-lined apartment on the Boulevard Haussmann so that intrusive noise would not disturb his delicate concentration. By contrast, the American positively enjoyed discomfort, noise and danger. His best moments, even his most euphoric ones, seem to have come when being rained upon by mortars, gored by fighting bulls, sniped at with bullets or as a passenger in a crashing plane.

So it is interesting that Hemingway disdained a writer's chair. Wherever it may be, the sitting position can have a profound effect on mood and performance. The reason you never want to turn right on a plane is that aircraft always approach the jetway on the port side because the captain sits on the left and it's his job to do the parking, a task that even in the automated age is largely old-world mechanics and hand–eye coordination. So, the doors are on the left. First Class is always at the front of the plane because it's smoother and quieter there. And thus, the directional imperative about how to enter an aircraft. First Class is lovely if you like smoked salmon roulades, but might it be more *interesting* in the cramped and noisy aft, somewhere near the toilets?

A certain amount of discomfort may be beneficial. Proust was a semi-permanent invalid and, while he lived in fine *haut bourgeois* material comfort, his disabling ailments might have contributed to his style. There is even some medical evidence that tuberculosis might have a directly stimulating effect: certainly, the history of Romantic literature with its cast of tragic, consumptive geniuses supports this.

More generally, strangeness and disruption, including Hemingway's explosives, are reliable stimulants. As Hunter S. Thompson observed, 'When the going gets weird, the weird turn pro.' And then he added perhaps a little mournfully: 'It never got weird enough for me.' At least until he died, when his final wish was carried out by his executor, Johnny Depp: Thompson's ashes were shot into space by a rocket.

There's not a lot more disruptive than death, but before the event, contemplation of it does help concentrate the mind rather wonderfully: here we have the ultimate deadline and it's clearly best to get things done before it's too late. Arbitrary violence can be helpful too. The boxer Mike Tyson said: 'Everyone has a plan . . . until they are punched in the mouth.' That's a fine demonstration of uncomfortable events inspiring a creative change of tack.

We are perverted by the idea of creative turmoil and how distress can stimulate and how change is always necessary, but many successful civilisations valued none of these things. Confucianism, for example, preferred stability and tradition to disruption and innovation. Yet the powerful residue of this fine culture may yet inhibit the evolution of creativity in modern China. For all its economic and industrial achievements, modern China has yet to innovate . . . in any field.

But what can be said of the place of comfort and delight in creativity? Not all accidents are calamities: the happy accident can be a productive one. And the word for a happy accident is 'Serendipity', a creative coinage of Horace Walpole in 1754. The word first appears in a letter the Prime Minister's dilettante son wrote to Horace Mann, a Grand Tour socialite who kept open house at the Palazzo Moretti in Florence.

The reference is to the Three Princes of Serendip and Walpole's source was Michele Tramezzino's *Peregrinaggio di tre giovani figliuoli del re de Serenedippo* (1557), a Venetian fable which was itself inspired by Firdawsi's classic Persian fairy-tale the *Shanameh*. As a man of leisure who lived in great comfort at Strawberry Hill, his Gothic fantasy near Twickenham, Walpole had time, opportunity and inclination to consider a wide range of sources for his meditations.

The story is convoluted but essentially the three young princes have to identify a lost camel they have never actually seen, but by accepting accidents, they get their result. From this small, but nice, fable, Walpole gave us an entire creative construct, the whimsical, delightful 'Serendipity'.

This is a comfortable condition. By definition, serendipity requires no ungentlemanly effort, no irritable pursuit of anything, still less exposure to danger. All you need to do is abandon existing prejudices and leave your mind open to chance . . . perhaps in the comfort of a seductively plush chair.

The child is father of the man

▶ **We talk about creativity as if it's something we can conjure out of the ether by some rational, adult stratagem. A brainstorming session would be a good example of this type of activity. Yet the truth is that creativity is hard-wired within us, almost certainly from a very early age.**

There are adult disciplines we can use to release that creative flair (and brainstorming isn't one of them, but that's another chapter). However, these disciplines depend on there being a solid foundation of imaginative talent on which to build. That talent is shaped in childhood, and our childhood experiences stay with us forever and shape how we are as adults.

Here's an interesting, though distressing, example. René Magritte was one of the most brilliant artists of the surrealist movement. His provocative images have become famous across the globe: everyday images tweaked in an unexpected way into something sinister. Consider for instance his painting *Les Amants*, which you can see on the following page.

We see two lovers, or so the title tells us, facing the artist almost as if posing for a shot to go on Facebook. But their heads are shrouded in cloth – for no apparent reason. The effect is strange and unsettling. Why are they like this? What does it signify?

It's an image which evokes dark and troubled emotions. But those emotions suddenly become much darker still when we read that

Les Amants, **René Magritte**

Magritte's mother drowned herself when Magritte was only thirteen. When her body was found in the river, her head was shrouded by her dress.

Knowing about the painter's mother and the circumstances of her suicide makes it impossible to look at the painting without feeling a cold frisson.

Magritte painted many versions of this image: it was a theme to which he returned again and again. Clearly, the artist is not painting what he wants to paint: he is painting what he has to paint. He is struggling to exorcise the ghosts of his childhood.

Another artist whose work owes more than you might expect to childhood experience is the fashion photographer Helmut Newton: though it seems almost dismissive to call him just a 'fashion photographer' as his work transcended the limits of the genre, turning it into a kind of surrealist art form. He is celebrated for glamorous images of beautiful and sexy women, often naked, and always in settings of great style – expensive hotels, yachts in the Mediterranean and so on.

But these women are not the vulnerable, waif-like, almost anorexic young girls we expect to see in so much modern fashion photography. On the contrary, they are mature, sophisticated, often buxom women, and they appear very much in control. Indeed one of his books was titled *Big Nudes* and it was exactly that – images of statuesque, confident, domineering women.

A Newton woman is never some malleable bimbo. Rather the reverse, she seems confident, strong and very much in charge of the situation. And that situation will, typically, be a yacht off the Mediterranean coast, an elegant apartment in Paris, a luxury hotel in Los Angeles or the Cote d'Azur. These strong women were always seen in a background of extravagance and glamour.

You might imagine that Newton photographed these powerful women simply because he found them sexually attractive. Indeed that was the assumption of many of his feminist critics. (And there were plenty of those.) As for his tendency always to use the most glamorous of locations, well, why not?

But if you dig into Newton's early life, a very different explanation offers itself. He was born in Berlin in 1920, into a very rich Jewish family. He was educated to luxury from early days: he had his own nanny, and was taken to school in a chauffeur-driven limousine. His mother was very much the 'grande dame', a handsome, extravagantly dressed and powerful figure, both physically and emotionally. She was the driving force in the Neustädter (as it was then) household.

Then, in 1938, everything collapsed. The persecution of the Jews in Berlin was intensifying horribly. Helmut's parents feared for their lives, and for their children's. They decided to flee to South America, but a whole family was too obvious a target, so the eighteen-year-old Helmut was given a ticket to Shanghai, and made to flee on his own. It's hard to imagine a more terrifying and traumatising lurch into adult life.

Knowing this, we need to look again at Newton's work. His own mother presented him with a powerful role model of a strong and confident woman. So it is reasonable to speculate that his preference in adult life to photograph forceful, proud women may, at a subconscious level, owe much to the memory of his mother. The richly glamorous settings of his shots are also perhaps more than a fashion backdrop: are they not symptoms of Newton casting back nostalgically to the pre-Nazi luxury of his childhood, before the brutality of Hitler's regime snatched everything away from him?

So Magritte had his mother taken away by fate; and Newton had his family and his whole way of life taken from him by fate. As adults, both of these artists clearly drew on the pain of their childhoods as creative inspiration for their art.

The art & craft & taste of memory

One of the great preoccupations of the Renaissance was the 'art of memory'. Or maybe it was a craft. Anyway, it was believed that memory could (and should) be trained. A Jesuit from Macerata called Matteo Ricci left Italy for China in 1577. On arrival, he introduced the Bible to the Ming Dynasty, but also taught the Emperors how to think in the European fashion.

Ricci's other export besides the Holy Book was the Memory Palace. This was a curious intellectual device which, should you need to remember something, required you to visualise the architectural plan of a large palazzo and to leave an idea in every room. When the ideas needed to be retrieved, you simply took an imaginative walk around the building, picking up cerebral memories as you went. Of course, taking a walk in a different direction, the sequence of memories would be different. Maybe this is what it means to change your mind: to attack a problem, or a palace, differently.

Savour all the meanings and metaphors of the expression 'changing your mind'. There are days when this seems a delightful prospect. Not just a modest alteration in opinions, but a complete refit. Keynes said: 'When my information changes, I alter my conclusions.'

In his Berggasse apartment in Vienna's 9th District, Sigmund Freud collected antique sculptures and bibelots that helped him confirm the connection between his own modern ideas and the past.

This cabinet of curios was a museum of memory. Through Freud's collection, disturbed Vienna was given a classical gloss. It was literally the Archaeology of Thought: artefacts as prompts to creativity. Of course, so much of Freud's theories is about suppressed memories. So much the better if a little Greek *kouros* could trigger them.

Changing your mind is a very good way to prove you actually have one. Freud changed his in spectacular fashion when he reversed out of his position on Seduction Theory. Significantly, no loss in professional status was involved in so public a repudiation of a belief that was central to his thought. Creative people always believe they can get a better idea and a change of mind is often the means to that end.

When Marcel Proust changed his mind, it led to (*a*) one of literature's greatest descriptions of memory (what he called *l'édifice du souvenir*) and (*b*) one of literature itself's greatest achievements, the roman-fleuve *In Search of Lost Time* (1913, English translation 1922–31).

Significantly, food was involved in the triggering of Proust's memory. There's a neurological explanation for this: our reaction to food is largely determined by aroma and the part of the brain that processes smell is a neighbour to the part that processes memory. Clearly, ideas leak. This is why for many people the smell of overcooked cabbage will forever suggest school. Perhaps Freud also enjoyed autonomous insights over his customary torte at Vienna's smoke-filled Café Landtmann.

But the evidence about food being a stimulus to creativity is mixed, or even contrary. The ancient Greeks had a frugal, charmless and harsh diet based on gruel and porridge. Breakfast might be flatbread with lentils and they drank their wine diluted. Heracles himself performed his great labours on a diet of mashed beans. True, the Spartans ate a vigorous black soup made of pig's blood, but they were

always exceptional. Anyway, this diet was no deterrent to high creativity: it gave us Pericles and Socrates.

Meanwhile, contemporary Brooklyn can offer craft beer, turmeric
latte, hazelnut and barberry granola, bio-dynamic wine, lobster with
kabocha squash, charred broccolini with cashews, Spanish mackerel
with ponzu and yolk jam, quail with toffee mayo or beets with black
sesame tahini and . . . it has only given us hipsters who knit their own
trousers and wear Napapijri hoodies.

Anyway, Proust and his mind change. He was thinking of a late
afternoon snack and, hesitant, he decides to go for the decoction of
lime blossom after all. This, triggering a memory, inspired the most
wonderful riff about . . . creativity. It appears in volume 1 of the Scott
Moncrieff translation: 'Overture'.

Returning home, Marcel's mother offered him some tea, a drink he
did not normally take. He dithered and then decided, hell, why ever
not? Mother then also ordered up a madeleine, one of those little
cakes 'which look as though they had been moulded in the fluted
valve of a scallop shell'.

He crumbled some of the madeleine into the tea. As he raised his
cuppa, Marcel reflected on the dreary day he had just spent and his
depressing prospects for the day after. And then there was a bit of
Eureka!

No sooner had the warm liquid mixed with the crumbs touched my palate than a shudder ran through me and I stopped, intent on the extraordinary thing that was happening to me.

Marcel found that an exquisite pleasure was invading his senses. It
was an isolated and detached sensation, which, immediately,
reminded him of nothing he recognised. Except, that is, pure

pleasure. And this was transformative: 'And at once the vicissitudes of life had become indifferent to me, its disasters innocuous, its brevity illusory.' He describes the sense of being in touch with a special essence . . . but a special essence which had completely overwhelmed him. In fact, become him. And he stopped feeling mediocre and mortal.

He sensed the taste might have been the stimulus, but 'the truth I am seeking lies not in the cup, but in myself'. So he put down his cup and began to examine his own mind, a process that led to (and underpinned) the creation of his amazing masterpiece. And Marcel realised he was not simply seeking something, but rather . . . creating it.

And he described creativity as being vis-à-vis with something that does not yet exist. So that nothing could interrupt his inward journey, he shut out all noise.

And as he concentrated, he felt something rise within him, like an anchor coming up from a great depth. 'I can hear the echo of great spaces traversed,' he says, and then writes his most famous passage:

But when from a long-distant past nothing subsists, after the people are dead, after the things are broken and scattered, taste and smell alone, more fragile but more enduring, more unsubstantial, more persistent, more faithful, remain poised a long time, like souls, remembering, waiting, hoping, amid the ruins of all the rest; and bear unflinchingly, in the tiny and almost impalpable drop of their essence, the vast structure of recollection.

There's an instructive YouTube video of Martha Stewart making madeleines. You need unsalted butter, flour, lemon zest, eggs, vanilla, a little salt and quite a lot of sugar. Ingredients alone cannot explain creativity . . . but can, evidently, inspire it.

When Proust experienced that collision of taste and memory, he began an internal journey. Although no physical dangers were involved, this was a journey undertaken with bravery, astonishing concentration and absolute commitment. And it was a journey that discovered buried treasure.

All poets depend on memory. Dante saw Beatrice when he was only nine and she never left his imagination. Wordsworth's 'natural presences' were inspired by childhood memories. And Stephen Spender averred: 'the imagination itself is an exercise of memory'. And memories of taste might be imagination's greatest stimulant.

Sex: St Augustine's autonomous penis

Creativity is a rush of blood to the head. And perhaps elsewhere too. St Thomas Aquinas believed that sex 'loosened the human spirit'. Indeed it does. It puts us on imaginative vectors. And while on imaginative vectors, discoveries may be made.

After the initial Act of Creation, procreation followed: the baton of creativity was passed to mortals, a Christian equivalent of the Prometheus fire-stealing myth. By way of introduction to a new world of possibilities, the Serpent says to Eve in the Garden of Eden: 'Your eyes will be opened.' Indeed, they were. Sex requires imagination, energy and courage.

Reveries of one sort or another are often fertile ground for creative thought. Mary Shelley let her mind go blank and allowed the story that became *Frankenstein* to take its place in the emptiness. And sex is the most productive reverie of them all. Sexual success requires creative stratagems and, for most of us, the prospect of sexual delight is a continuous stimulant.

Sex is, obviously, a defining creative act, both practical and metaphysical. The mating patterns of eels in the Sargasso Sea may illustrate an ineluctable biological imperative, but since Eden, culture has, to put it no more emphatically, tended to dissociate pleasure from matter-of-fact reproduction. We have, or at least most of us have, moved beyond mere biological urges. As Chaucer said of

Chauntecleer (a randy cock serving a clear symbolic purpose in *The Nun's Priest's Tale*): his lusty actions were 'more for delyt than world to multiplye'.

A splendid example of this was known to Boccaccio. He makes a reference to the Saracen princess Alatiel, daughter of the Sultan of Babylon, who had sex no fewer than ten thousand times with eight busy lovers in a mere four years. Clearly, more activity than was strictly necessary for family maintenance. Alatiel – and one longs to know the creative details of the presentation – ambitiously offered herself to the King of the Algarve as a virgin bride.

Creative self-expression and self-identity are, thus, also involved in sex. As is competition. In every case, vibrations in the groin may feed into vibrations of the mind because sex is 'the reflex of our earthly frame', according to Coleridge. So sex has its place in any account of creativity. As if to confirm, a website shrieks 'Boost Your Sex Life With These Creative Ideas'. A silly listicle follows:

1. **Dress to impress. (Possible Interpretation: change your kebab-smeared, greying T-shirt for . . .)**
2. **Give her specific compliments.**
3. **Kiss like you mean it. (Possible Interpretation: none of this miserable dry pecking . . .)**
4. **Send flirtatious texts.**
5. **Give in to temptation.**
6. **Let her catch you staring.**

But what really stimulates sexual desire? Response is initiated by a scale running, in descending order, from beautiful, enticing, fascinating, adorable, alluring, covetable, fetching, plain, repulsive to disgusting. Tastes differ, but in most cases, it is beauty (no matter how difficult to define) that is most positively exciting. This matter occupied theorists of art in the Renaissance. When a Neoplatonist saw a beautiful body, his thoughts might turn to divine inspiration, sensing that the beauty perceived might be an indication of the presence of God. The result was a sort of divine madness . . . which was a good thing. This was another term for arousal. And arousal leads to action, either mechanical or metaphysical. A graphic of this process would explain a great deal about the emotional dynamics of humanity.

Desire may be the motivational driver, but the relationship of sexual desire to beauty is not straightforward – very little to do with sexual desire is. As W. H. Auden knew, 'The desires of the heart are as crooked as corkscrews.' Or Vladimir Nabokov's 'hidden tumour of an unspeakable passion', which he mentions in *Lolita*, his paedophile novel of 1955. Here, disease in the form of a tumour is a metaphor of desire, as it often is in discussions of artistic creation. And today, Lolita might be unpublishably illegal on account of its beautiful advocacy of sex with under-age girls.

Still, it is great art. Nabokov again: 'Every movement she made, every shuffle and ripple, helped me to conceal and improve the secret

system of tactile correspondence between beast and beauty – between my gagged, bursting beast and the beauty of her dimpled body in its innocent cotton frock.' Only the brain dead would not find that exciting.

But here's a laboratory truth: depression blocks desire.

In a paper published by the American Psychological Association, Gayle Beck of the University of Houston explained that in an experiment, men listening to recordings of sex were, not at all surprisingly, stimulated by the sounds of slap, tickle, slurp, moan and sigh, but inhibited if they sensed fear in the recording. For the lab rats, the slap, tickle and so on was a stimulus both in the conceptual and mechanical senses. Conceptually, they wished to be taking part. Mechanically, they entertained, in the area of the groin, what is politely called genital arousal.

The scientific view is simple. The immense cultural construct we call Love is a product of brain chemistry, which takes the form of a neurotransmitter. This is Dopamine, or 3,4-dihydroxyphenethylamine. It is found in banana peel and also in the brains of individuals whose thought patterns are turning towards sex.

Sex, of course, stimulates great poetry and art. John Donne dreamt of the pubic triangle in frank terms:

> **Off with your wiry coronet and show**
> **The hairy diadem which on you doth grow.**

And here is Mario Vargas Llosa describing the same territory:

> **The scent of vanilla that suggests the rich treasure**
> **of warmth and moistures of her private parts . . .**
> **like a whiff of overripe cheese.**

Just the thought of these cross-over sensations drives him to 'blissful, intoxicated rapture'. And possibly then to future creative reaction . . . such as writing a beautiful book.

Never mind modern novelists of the greatest distinction, the Church Fathers gave sex an unusual amount of attention. St Augustine, though a youth of splendid inhibition, became something of an expert in carnal matters. Sex became for him more than a pumping and squirting expression of lust, but a demonstration of free will. Or, indeed, the want of it.

Through thoughtful and practical experiment, Augustine discovered that the penis is the only body part which not merely defies the control of the will, but actually had a more or less ungovernable will of its own. St Augustine's unruly penis was a metaphor not so much of the Holy Spirit as of the creative spirit. It is a short step to seeing that artistic production is an expression of sexual potency. And writer's block . . . may be the opposite.

In St Augustine's case, sexual desire inspired what Rebecca West described as 'the most intense experience ever commemorated'. This is nicely rendered by Sarah Ruden in her translation of *The Confessions* (2017). The experience involved St Augustine and his mother, Monica: 'stretching upward with a more fiery emotion' they felt themselves climbing ever higher, through all the degrees of matter and through the heavenly spheres and, higher still, to the regions of their own souls and up toward the eternity that lies beyond time itself. Rarely can mothers have encouraged such creativity.

But what is this about 'beyond time itself'? It is reminiscent of the French for orgasm: *petit mort*. Maybe the ultimate pleasure is to escape sensations and time.

The IIEF or International Index of Erectile Function (which shares its abbreviation with the Indonesian International Education Foundation) is based on data collected from a questionnaire (irresistible not to describe it as penetrating in its thoroughness) asking

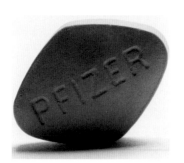

hapless correspondents to calculate hardness, frequency of ejaculation and duration or intensity of pleasure. If any device could be calculated to be a sexual deterrent this, surely, would be it.

But sildenafil citrate might be a remedy. And sexual adventure might be creativity's fellow traveller . . . at least for a part of the journey. Sildenafil citrate was formulated in Pfizer's laboratories in Sandwich, Kent in 1998. Originally intended as a remedy for hypertension, as 'Viagra' it became one of the great branding exercises in modern business. This little blue pill, analogous to the purple heart amphetamines of the Vietnam era, has enhanced the blood flow to billions of penises, which are now more readily available than heretofore to demonstrate the throbbing mechanics of desire. And possibly stimulating more creative patterns of thought the while.

And Viagra proves that desire for sex, as does desire for other things, must exist in the future rather than the here and now. It needs to be taken not more than four hours and not less than thirty minutes before anticipated sex. What a fascinating window that is.

The paradoxes of sex are made clear by this drug. It does not increase yearning and has no therapeutic effect on those not actually needing treatment for fundamental erectile dysfunction. Happily, it has been shown to increase the shelf-life of cut flowers and aids recovery of jet lag in hamsters (at least, according to some Argentinian researchers).

Which brings us to Pier Paolo Pasolini's idea that sex is a consolation for misery. And misery drives us on, creatively speaking.

To produce a good idea, start from a bad place

It's widely assumed that to produce a good idea, one must first get into a good space emotionally. But in reality the opposite is true. It is often bad situations which inspire good solutions. A great setback can be the spur for a great leap forward, while good situations are more likely to encourage complacency than creativity.

Here's an example. It's centred on a young man called Oskar Barnack who, one hundred years ago, was working for Leitz, a German lens manufacturer. Barnack's life was dominated by two forces. The first of these was a great passion for landscape photography. But in those days, a camera was a big and cumbrous apparatus, with large plates instead of film, and a bulky wooden tripod. That was a nuisance for any photographer, but it was more than a nuisance for Barnack: it was a medical risk. Because the second great force in Barnack's life was that he suffered from severe asthma. As a consequence, any journey into the countryside with the heavy photographic equipment of the time might well trigger a potentially fatal asthma attack.

This huge handicap provoked Barnack to think that there must be a better way. And he noticed in the cinema that a large and wondrous image could be projected on the screen from a tiny strip of film, only 35 mm wide. If that worked for the cinema, why not for still photography?

He worked with his colleagues at Leitz to make a tiny camera, using 35-mm cine film. Progress was delayed by the First World War, but in 1925 the 'Leitz camera' – abbreviated to 'Leica' – was launched. Little bigger than a man's hand, its compactness enabled a much quicker, more spontaneous approach to image-making, and this transformed photography forever.

Many of the twentieth century's greatest photographers, from Cartier-Bresson to Elliott Erwitt to Sebastião Salgado, used a Leica. Many of the century's most famous images were shot on a Leica. It was an innovation that revolutionised the way we see things.

Yet it's a revolution that might never have happened if Oscar Barnack hadn't had the misfortune to suffer from asthma.

The story of the Leica camera shows that great things can emerge from weakness. You can see the same phenomenon, on a much grander scale, in recent history. After the Second World War, the nations of Germany and Japan were not just defeated but crushed. Yet by the 1970s, they had been reborn as two of the most powerful economies on earth – while one victor, America, toiled tragically in Vietnam, and another, Great Britain, struggled to make sense of life without an empire.

L'appel du vide: the sublime, risk & danger

Imagine walking along a disturbingly tall parapet. Perhaps in a tricky wind. It is horrible but delicious simultaneously. Like a rooftopper, that new urban tribe which scales impossibly tall buildings unaided. The popularity of their YouTube video accounts shows that we all take voyeuristic pleasure from scary spectacles. Who has not known the peculiar thrill of peering nervously out of an open window high above the ground?

Standing on the tracks in front of a fast-approaching train is a reliable, if risky, way of stimulating thought. Especially thoughts about survival. Adrenalin and exaggerated heart rate are, in these circumstances, reliably exciting. All experiences of speed seem to have endocrinological effects, which people find generally pleasing. In this way, the body's alarm circuits work like muses.

Driving fast, you sometimes think a flick of a wheel and you could hit that truck. You stare up or down stairwells. You toy with the idea of opening the plane door. Or imagine something else really scary like going to Stansted Airport, an experience so horrible it is richly provocative of imaginative fantasies about better places to be and better things to do. If you push, you get somewhere, according to Newton's Laws of Motion.

Psychologists use the term High Place Phenomenon to describe that strange cocktail of fascination and terror experienced when walking along a precipitous cliff edge or a mountain pass. And the French, in that French way, have an even better and more poetic term for it. This is *'l'appel du vide'*, literally 'the call of the void'. Intrepid cliff walkers are always drawn ever nearer to the edge, toying with an irrational urge to fling themselves into oblivion.

The reason why a healthy person enjoying a cliff or mountain walk should flirt with elective death is not that they harbour occult thoughts about suicide. In fact, quite the opposite. The reason we experience *l'appel du vide* is because flirting with death has nothing to do with self-sabotage. Rather, it confirms the will to live. The overwhelming majority of people who experience *l'appel* and who even seek it out ignore the call. It is simply necessary to have heard it.

That fear is delicious is an idea with origins in the classical past, but became a principle of Enlightenment aesthetics, most famously in Edmund Burke's treatise *A Philosophical Enquiry into the Origin of Our Ideas of the Sublime and the Beautiful* (1757). Burke's 'sublime' is 'whatever is fitted in any sort to excite the ideas of pain and danger'.

The concept of masochism did not exist in Burke's day – we had to wait for a troubled Viennese novelist, Leopold von Sacher-Masoch, to put his name to it – but Burke was not advocating self-harm. Instead, people should become 'conversant about terrible objects' (including craggy peaks, chasms, wild animals and storms) so as to enjoy them, because fear is stimulating and terror is pleasurable. Burke believed that the sublime was the most intense feeling any individual might experience.

Today's horror movies with chainsaws, predatory sharks, burning buildings, cosmic collisions, rats, spiders and serial killers have their origin in this current of eighteenth-century thought. Burke's contemporaries included the actor David Garrick, whose performance as the title character in the Drury Lane production of *Macbeth* made, by contemporary accounts, the audience's skin crawl. But this sensation of creeping flesh was widely enjoyed. At the same time, the Gothic novels of Horace Walpole and Ann Radcliffe titillated their readers with rattling windows, cries of women in pain, lightning and dark spaces.

We enjoy horror and creative people will always look for edges, wherever they may be found and whether they are real or metaphorical. But just as anyone hearing *l'appel du vide* will never actually answer the call, those edges can never be discovered. They are not there to be discovered, only to be sought out. As Hunter S. Thompson knew:

The Edge . . . there is no honest way to explain it because the only people who really know where it is are ones who have gone over.

How to Steal Fire

Fear and desire are as curiously linked as pleasure and pain. To understand fear, you need first to be on nodding terms with the concepts of Hebbian synaptic plasticity and at ease with your ionotropic glutamate receptors. Or, perhaps more agreeably, to read Manhattan boulevardier-novelist Jay McInerney, who says: 'Sometimes I think the difference between what we want and what we are afraid of is about the width of an eyelash.' We can be frightened by what we want.

And what we enjoy most can become a source of dread: Shakespeare had this conceit about weeping to have that which we fear to lose. The idea that desire and fear may be linked as psychological opposites, on the same cerebral circuit as addiction and phobia, was reinforced by a 2008 University of Michigan research project showing that changing stress levels can make the brain immediately flip from pleasant desire to unsettling dread.

Stanley Kubrick's first film, shown at New York's Guild Theater in 1953, was *Fear and Desire*. Survivors emerge from a plane that's crashed in an unidentified war zone. It was shot without sound on a low budget, and a child's pram was used in place of a professional cinema track and dolly. James Agee told Kubrick that the film had 'too many good things . . . to call [it] arty'.

Repulsion is the mirror image of desire. Repulsion is based not on a future-perfect yearning, but on historic knowledge of what is disagreeable. Phobia makes this more subtle since, like desire, it projects into the future.

Like desire, phobia can be defined in terms of anticipation, but anticipation not of pleasure but of dread. Just as the yearning for a Porsche projects the imagination beyond the here and now into some pleasant future state where roads are empty, bank account ample and the sun always shining, so a phobia derives its horrible strength from a fear of what might happen. We might be trapped in a lift or have an encounter with spiders.

But we do not need to know about ionotropic glutamate receptors or monoamine neuromodulatory mechanisms, or any of the other hormones fired by our alarm circuits. We simply need to know that danger and fear, crisis, menace, perils and threats are powerful stimulants.

And the fire stealer now needs to ask: if danger, fear, crisis, menace, peril and threat are good for us, or for our creativity, then how might we get more of them? You could climb to the top of the building, put a gun to your head and ask that very question. Or you could, metaphorically speaking, jump off a cliff and see if you sprout wings on the descent.

The discomfort zone

When I was running my own advertising agency, I was preoccupied by two anxieties. First, would our clients accept and publish the creative ideas we produced to help them sell their products? Without that, there would be nothing. Second, would our ideas be genuinely original and distinctive? I saw little point in putting my life savings at risk and working endless hours if we were not producing work we could be proud of.

It's hard to judge either of these two questions. You only know for sure whether the client will buy the campaign idea once he's seen it – and then it's too late. And it's near to impossible to judge one's own work: no mother thinks she has an ugly baby.

I learnt to apply a simple but paradoxical test. In that nervous gap between the idea being drafted and showing it to the client, I'd ask myself if I was a bit scared of presenting it. Did I fear he might turn it down? If I did have that fear (and this is where the paradox comes in) then I'd decide that the idea was distinctive enough. If I thought it would be easy to sell, I'd hesitate about showing it. That sounds the wrong way round, but there is a logic to it.

People are generally a bit frightened of new ideas until they've had time to get used to them. But unremarkable ideas aren't threatening, so they're easy to accept. Which means that if you feel comfortable with an idea at first glance, it's probably a bit anodyne. Conversely, if it makes you feel uneasy, there may well be something potent in it.

The lesson is simple: to judge an idea, ask yourself if it falls in your comfort zone, or does it find a kind of new discomfort zone? If it makes you feel comfortable at first, it's a good bet it'll make you feel bored later. But if it's a bit scary the first time round, there may well be something in it which will grow on you.

It's important to understand that when a creative mind comes up with an innovative concept, they are not just producing a new idea, they are also rejecting the old ideas. And it's the old ideas, the familiar ones, that make us feel comfortable.

'If you're not a bit frightened, then you aren't going fast enough.'

So, if we're searching for ideas, it's crucial that we leave our comfort zone behind us, and learn to love our discomfort zone. As my instructor said to me when I spent a day learning how to drive a high-performance car round a race track, 'If you're not a bit frightened, then you aren't going fast enough.'

Desire

Desire is the sixth sense, at least according to Brillat-Savarin, the wisest of all writers on food. His *Physiologie du goût* is the source of that resonant truth: tell me what you eat and I will tell you what you are. To which the creative imagination adds the gloss: tell me *where* you eat and I will tell you what you want to be. Restaurants depend on this creative illusion.

The Tao belief that the important thing is the journey, not the arrival: that is the essence of desire. Gratification is not the object, instead it is more a matter of visualisation or fantasy. Desire is a prospector that maps the landscape of all our appetites. Like radar, it's a raster scan of possibilities, real and imagined.

The creative imagination is wide-angled and inclusive. This, Charles Eames said, is why cars have bigger windscreens than rear-view mirrors. Seeing where you are going is more important than reflecting on where you have been.

Desire is yearning and peering through that windscreen with a tangible but distant, even unattainable, focus. Craving is feral. Desire is cultivated. Desire may even be one of the defining characteristics of civilised life: the ability to project into the future.

Desire is creative because it is not a passive function but an active one. It is more subtle and complex than mere lust, although subtlety and complication are not everything. Lust is crude and unreflective, a spasm of the groin, not a troubadour's romantic strategy, or the

Romantic poet's hard true flame, or the yearning of Cole Porter. Desire is a function not just of the senses, but of the intellect as well. Lust may (or may sometimes not) be gratified immediately. Desire is continuous.

And desire is always in the future (while nostalgia is always in the past). It is a device for taking you somewhere else. And what excites desire? The ghost of a nipple under silk, the smell of a peach, the sound of a Ferrari, the taste of Krug '09, a sunset over the Aegean. And it is always so enigmatic: C. S. Lewis catches the sense of it: '. . . only the scent of a flower we have not found, the echo of a tune we have not heard, news from a country we have never yet visited'.

Because desire operates in the future, it sometimes causes disappointment in the present. As a long-range function, it's not always matched to the realities of the here and now. Like phantom limbs, men may remain desirous of women long after the technical means has escaped them because of atherosclerosis, diabetes or obesity. 'Is it not strange', Shakespeare writes in *Henry IV, Part II* 'that desire should so many years outlive performance?' A great deal of life's bittersweet poignancy is captured in that single line.

And in this finding too: a journalist set out to establish what was the 'normal' frequency of sex. The common assumption of three to four times a week was found, in a survey, to be more a pleasing fantasy than a statistical reality. In this way, the *New York Times* discovered that desire outpaced reality. Desire always does.

Desire may be the source of all practical and creative motivation: the human predicament might be described by our experience of it. We have a sense of an unrealised ideal, a feeling that our own life is imperfect or incomplete. The emotions thus aroused are ambivalent, but force us to reconsider our existing view of the world and perhaps to make imaginative modifications to it.

Plato wanted us to aim for something more elevated than desire because, he thought, desire keeps you trapped in the base, material world. But that's exactly the point: therein lie desire's pleasures and pains. Quite correctly, Spinoza thought desire a sort of slavery, although slavery, perhaps, of an enjoyable sort. The Buddhists still want us to put a stop to it since desire causes unhappiness (or, capitalists would say, excites motivation). One of the Four Noble Truths of Buddhism is that desire leads to *dukkha*, an existential suffering. Of course it does, but that same suffering encourages creative stratagems to avoid the misery. Or enjoy it en route.

One of Freud's most familiar concepts is *Wunscherfüllung im Traum*, or wish-fulfilment in dreams. This was writing about what has often been thought, but never so polysyllabically expressed. That's to say, the idea that the landscape of our dreams is one we want to will into existence. We dream, by night or day, about places we want to be. Except, of course, if it's a bad dream. But Freud would, in his incorrigible way, insist that a bad dream is itself the result of confused, or repressed, desire.

In confirmation of a poetic idea, there is in Andrei Tarkovsky's dark 1979 film *The Stalker* a secret room where desires are satisfied. In a rather laboured visual metaphor, the heroes are led through a Zone before access to the ultimate goal: a pleasure centre where desires can be realised. Alas, in a gruesome footnote, Tarkovsky's death seems to have been caused by the inhalation of deadly toxins while filming on location in Lithuania. The pursuit of desire can be dangerous.

At this stage, it probably needs to be said, in an uncomplicated way, that desire is concerned with the identification and capture of pleasure. Its own dynamic is a graphic of sex's familiar bell curve with climax and collapse. It's the culture of our appetites, our most positive and pleasurable yearnings. We can bring Freud on again. His *Wunsch* is the pleasure-seeking mechanism that dominates our egos. His disciple Jacques Lacan translated *Wunsch* as *désir*. And Lacan defined desire as what remains when you subtract momentary lust from eternal love. Julian Barnes identified the same conceptual territory, but described it differently. For Barnes, pleasure comes first in the form of anticipation and second in the form of memory.

Appetite is the first stirring of desire. And it's a very good idea to cultivate it: 'Those who restrain desire, do so because theirs is weak enough to be restrained,' according to William Blake. Maybe Henry James suffered from weak desire when he said it was like hunger, being morbid, sterile and hateful.

But appetite does not only apply to food. We have appetites for travel as well, what the Germans call *Wanderlust*. Stendhal Syndrome was defined in 1979 by Graziella Magherini after a reading of *Naples and Florence: A Journey from Milan to Reggio*, wherein Stendhal describes the palpitations and 'celestial sensations' he experienced in front of Santa Croce. It was an anticipation of happiness and that's the ever-present subtext of desire.

Central to the idea of exotic travel is that gratification exists in another place, somewhere that is, by definition, not here: Auden's 'sunburnt otherwhere'. And this is a place where everyone is better looking, more tanned, where they have better sex, drink wine at all hours and are generally just one step away from a delirium of pleasure. This is anticipation: a pleasing speculation about some future good, a way of ameliorating the present.

Then the erotic pull of food cannot be ignored as a stimulus. There is a marvellous passage by Mario Vargas Llosa which says in the hour of love we experience:

> **tender abundance that appears to be just about to overflow yet remains firm, supple, resilient as ripe fruit and freshly kneaded dough, that soft texture Italians call *morbidezza*, a word that sounds lustful even when applied to bread.**

It goes beyond bread. Textures and colours and smells, sights and sounds, all service desire. Each can start an imaginative process. And what is most significant is that this process itself is the end and aim: 'Ultimately, it is the desire, not the desired, that we love,' according to Nietzsche.

Desire is a motivator, but can cause confusion. The veteran *New Yorker* journalist E. B. White said: 'I arise in the morning torn between a desire to improve . . . the world and a desire to enjoy . . . the world. This makes it hard to plan the day.' And this may be a nearly universal experience. Desire cannot be satisfied. It is an unappeasable want. And it moves us on. It makes us think, fantasise, yearn, calculate and regret.

That's why it helps us steal fire. Who doesn't admire that Tolstoy character who says I'd much prefer to have to say *I wish I hadn't*, than to be always thinking *I wish I had*?

Opium, drugs & drink: the booze muse

▶ **What's the role of intoxication in creation? By every account, opium dreams involve intense colours and excite powerful, often harrowing, visions. In both Poe and de Quincey, habitual abusers, a recurrent motif is a terrifying version of space limitlessly vast but claustrophobically controlled.**

But as Alethea Hayter says in *Opium and the Romantic Imagination* (1968), her classic study of narcotics and literature, while 'the action of opium may unbare some of the semi-conscious processes by which literature begins to be written', it is actually rather difficult to recall, still less describe, the intensity of the effect when sober. So, opium flatters only to deceive.

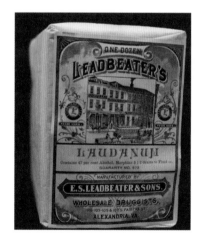

She gives examples. The most accessible version of opium was laudanum, a suspension of the drug in alcohol. Both Walter Scott and Wilkie Collins, neither committed junkies, dosed themselves with the tincture to help write when unwell. Thus *The Bride of Lammermoor* and *The Moonstone*, sober monuments to Victorian genius, were drug-fuelled masterpieces written by middle-aged men who were off their heads. The narcotics helped them write, but neither Scott nor Collins could remember anything about the experience.

Sobriety was never of much interest to hardcore Romantics, as opposed to professional gentleman writers. Indeed, the idea that sobriety is a benefit at all is historically specific and a largely modern conceit. Most of Byron's poetry was written on 'hock and soda-water', a mild potation when compared to Coleridge's Kendal Black Drop, which contained opium, vinegar, spices and sugar. Byron helpfully noted that his friend's tipple makes you 'drunk at once'. John Keats had a well-developed taste for claret, the experience of which he liked to enhance by putting black pepper on his tongue.

The evidence is clear that drugs and drink help generate imagery and ideas, but do little to help capture, describe or edit them. Nor are they ever a substitute for natural talent, only a potential accelerator of it, and that last is unproved. Substance abuse is an imperfect cicerone.

After experimenting with mescaline and describing his experiences in *The Doors of Perception* (1954), a title creatively thieved from William Blake, Aldous Huxley became unconvinced that drugs helped creativity. In an interview about LSD with the *Paris Review* in 1960 he said: 'You could never hope to reproduce to the full extent the quite incredible intensity of colour that you get under the influence of the drug.'

But he was impressed by the way LSD transformed his vision of the world. While under the influence, Huxley had *the impression* of experiencing 'penetrating insights' into both others and himself. He thought it was both cheaper and faster than psychotherapy in helping excavate buried personal material, which could be useful in writing.

LSD, Huxley thought:

> . . . **shows that the world one habitually lives in is merely a creation of this conventional, closely conditioned being which one is, and that there are quite other kinds of worlds outside. It's a very salutary thing to realize that the rather dull universe in which most of us spend most of our time is not the only universe there is.**

Still, the literature and art facilitated by LSD do not amount to much. The anthology of psychedelic creativity is a thin one: the fact remains that to describe a dream, you need to be awake, not zonked-out.

With alcohol, we are on more solid ground, although in this context that may be an absurd metaphor. There is ample evidence that alcohol facilitates painting and writing, even as its larger destructive effects are well known. William James, to suggest only one very singular example, admired alcohol because it was a votary of the 'Yes function in man'. And creativity is more closely allied with saying yes than with saying no. James it was who invented Pragmatism.

Take absinthe as an example. This was the fuel of nineteenth-century artistic Paris: the bohemian poet and painter sitting hollow-eyed in a cabaret with trembling lip and aesthetic pallor was, to be sure, an absinthe drinker. Besides simple drunkenness, of which it was a reliable cause, absinthe also caused vertigo, muscular spasms and narcosis. Its essential ingredient, alcohol apart, was wormwood, or *Artemisia absinthium*. In its purest form, oil of wormwood causes severe convulsions, blackout, constriction of the throat and, very likely, death.

These effects alone cannot explain its popularity. It excited both mania and fear: the first painting Edouard Manet submitted to the Paris Salon was *The Absinthe Drinker* in 1859. It shows a degenerate in a top hat. It scandalised the artistic establishment, who rejected it, eventually giving rise to the *Salon des Refusés* which, ironically, became far more significant than the Salon itself. Thus, in a round-about way, absinthe helped normalise the revolution of later nineteenth-century painting.

Two years before Manet, in *Les Fleurs du Mal*, Baudelaire claimed absinthe reversed the vectors of his poor and doomed soul. To Rimbaud the green fairy, *la fée verte,* was liquid alchemy, a drink that had a transforming effect on his imagination. Science, however, remains uncertain whether it was the daunting 80 per cent alcohol content of many commercial absinthes of Manet's day which had more effect than the presence of thujone, the psychoactive agent present in wormwood. Like a good curry, the green fairy also contained anise, fennel, coriander, marjoram, hyssop and *Calamus aromaticus*. Its sale was banned in France in 1914. Modern pastis is its house-trained descendant.

Despite being banned in 1912, legislation suggesting the existence of a problem, absinthe was never popular in the United States, but the following American Nobel Prize winners in Literature nonetheless managed to become hardcore alcoholics abusing only domestic liquor. Not, that is to say, mere bons viveurs with a taste for fine claret at dinner, but pitiable addicts with a destructive dependence pathology: Sinclair Lewis, Eugene O'Neill, William Faulkner, John Steinbeck and Ernest Hemingway. And, while not Nobel Laureates, the following distinguished themselves by being merely extremely heavy drinkers: Hart Crane, Edna St Vincent Millay, Thomas Wolfe, John Cheever, Norman Mailer, Djuna Barnes, Dorothy Parker and Hunter S. Thompson.

This is all delightfully explained in Tom Dardis's *The Thirsty Muse* (1989), an irreverent, but thoughtful, account of impressively creative drunks. Hemingway adapted O. Henry's witty remark that 'I drink to make other people amusing' and this ingenious strategy might account for much of alcohol's beneficial effect for the creative individual. Unamusing people may be transformed into useful material.

Hemingway's idiosyncratic and obsessive drink culture is explained by the founder of the Museum of the American Cocktail, Philip Greene, in *To Have and To Have Another* (2012). But a lot of Hemingway was ballyhoo and braggadocio. It is, for example, not at all clear that he much enjoyed drinking the cloudy mixture of champagne and absinthe which he recommended. Drink three to five . . . slowly, was his advice, and you will become agreeably drunk. However, always the one for practical advice, Papa insisted that while you may certainly 'write drunk', you must 'edit sober'.

So alcohol might offer a delusional fillip to creativity. It also has an uncertain role in matters of the heart. Shakespeare knew that drinking leads to 'nose-painting, sleep, and urine'. Porter says to Macduff,

Lechery, sir, it provokes, and unprovokes. It provokes the desire, but it takes away the performance. Therefore, much drink may be said to be an equivocator with lechery. It makes him, and it mars him . . . makes him stand to and not stand to.

But Hunter S. Thompson was more certain of the all-round benefits of intoxication. 'I hate', he said, 'to advocate drugs, alcohol, violence and insanity to anyone, but they've always worked for me.' He had a commitment to extremes in every activity. Of his motorbike he wrote: 'Faster, faster, faster, until the thrill of speed overcomes the fear of death.'

The opening passage of *Fear and Loathing in Las Vegas* (1972) has become a classic. Talking of the trunk of his signature '71 Chevrolet Impala convertible which he called the Great Red Shark, Thompson said:

We had two bags of grass, seventy-five pellets of mescaline, five sheets of high-powered blotter acid, a salt shaker half full of cocaine, and a whole galaxy of multi-colored uppers, downers, screamers, laughers . . . and also a quart of tequila, a quart of rum, a case of Budweiser, a pint of raw ether and two dozen amyls.

As is well known, in 1972 American cars had very big trunks. He modestly added: 'Not that we *needed* all that for the trip, but once you get locked into a serious drug collection, the tendency is to push it as far as you can.' Soon after Barstow, which is on Route 66 almost exactly halfway between Los Angeles and Las Vegas, which are a mere 270 miles apart, the drugs kicked in. But Thompson had many strategies to avoid incapacitation or even just hangovers.

His daily regime involved regular shots of Chivas Regal deluxe whisky, cocaine, marijuana, margaritas, beers, chartreuse and LSD. And to recover from benders he would breakfast on four Bloody Marys, two grapefruit, a pot of coffee, crêpes, a half-pound of non-specific 'meat' and a couple more margaritas. (The 'Bloody Mary', by the way, was created when Hemingway was hospitalised with war wounds and forbidden alcohol. The spicy tomato juice disguised the vodka and, at the time, Mary was his wife's name.)

In the absence of a supportive muse, artists crave other forms of stimulus. Coffee will do. At the same time as absinthe was wrecking one quarter of creative Paris, coffee became known as *le carburant des grands artistes* in another. Drinking coffee has always been a form of social promotion: Nescafé society is altogether more acceptable than crack dens, but coffee too has its dangers: 10 mg of caffeine within four to six hours may be fatal. Be that as it may, the prodigally industrious Balzac drank fifty coffees a day . . . although we do not know whether they were hearty mugs or cute, miniature *demi-tasses*.

And Balzac spoke very positively of its effects in 'The Pleasure and Pains of Coffee', an essay appearing in his *Traité des excitants modernes* (1838). It 'roasts your insides', Balzac said, although it was unclear why this was a good thing. He continued: 'Many people claim coffee inspires them, but . . . coffee only makes boring people more boring.' It is maybe this very act of *transformation*, from drabness to colour, from unamusing to amusing, from boring to even more boring, that makes drugs and drink (and coffee) such valuable accessories to creativity: the booze muse.

Avant-garde: *avant* to exactly what?

Being avant-garde – outraging conventions, debauching complacency, attacking the old order, being first – was once a reliable way to demonstrate exciting creative credentials.

In both science and art, novelty or invention, or neophilia, a sometimes crude infatuation with the slavish pursuit of the next-new-thing, became sovereign tests for quality of achievement. If it wasn't new, it couldn't be good. Creativity is, since Genesis, about making something *de novo ex nihilo*, or something new where nothing existed before.

For centuries, invention became the mother of necessity. That's an inversion of the old trope, but also very true. There's no rationality here, since creativity follows no predictable pattern. Often, inventions – especially cultural inventions – did not respond to any existing need . . . but actually created one. Obviously, such a process can lead to absurdities. For a while, novelty became an end in itself.

Still, our respect for creativity and innovation is so profound, it's tempting to regard it as instinctive, perhaps sourced in a racial memory of Eden. But maybe that moment is coming to an end. Perhaps now we are entering a long historical phase where consolidation of what is known is more valuable than the creation of what is merely new. Maybe old is better.

In literature, art and philosophy, provocative new movements have often been French in origin. Cubism, for example. Or the *nouveau roman* of Alain Robbe-Grillet and Nathalie Sarraute, who, all by themselves and without consultation with readers, decided that the realistic novel was *démodé*. Then there was nouvelle cuisine. No one could quite decide if its creative contrast of unusual tastes – smoked oyster with gooseberry, for example – was an anticipation of the brave new kitchen to come or a revival of depraved Roman flavour combos. Then there was the entire rag-bag of Post-Modernist 'thought', a perfect miniature of the avant-garde mentality.

Avant-garde is a revealing term because its source is military. The vanguard of an army was its leader, the brave shock troops who went into battle first, with a less exciting rearguard behind them. And a solid middle-guard in-between. The military metaphor suggests that culture is a battle, that progress is a necessity and to retreat a humiliation. But in both thinking and in art, the self-regarding avant-garde has recently suffered reversals. Perhaps because it was marching nowhere other than up its own *cul*.

It's, of course, a French term and much of what is conventionally considered avant-garde had its origins in peculiarly local Parisian traditions and practices. In the *grandes écoles* in the second half of the twentieth century, a new way of thinking about thinking evolved. Structuralism and Deconstruction set out to de-mythologise the rest of culture, while busily mythologising themselves.

The old mind–body dichotomy, which had been a feature of philosophy since Plato mused about shadows and caves, was no more. Meaning was relativised; the stable structure of language was questioned. Rather as Magritte had painted a pipe and titled the picture *Ceci n'est pas une pipe*, so a Deconstructionalist might question whether what you are reading is actually a book.

With Structuralism and Deconstruction, obscurity was often mistaken for profundity. It is impossible to determine any meaning in

Jacques Derrida's: 'To pretend, I actually do the thing. I have therefore pretended to pretend.' They used words like syntagmatic and paradigmatic, but until very recently no one questioned that avant-garde thought should be anything other than impenetrably meaningless. Generals in the *avant-garde* of the army opposed to old thinking included, as well as Derrida, Paul de Man, Jacques Lacan, Michel Foucault, Jean-François Lyotard, Luce Irigaray, Jean Baudrillard and Gilles Deleuze. Typical quote: 'postmodern [is an] incredulity toward metanarratives'. That's Lyotard, but it could have been any of the others' mumbo-jumbo too.

But then in 1997 an irreverent and mischievous physicist called Alain Sokal decided he had had enough of this baffling nonsense and wrote a book called *Intellectual Impostures*. Now avant-garde philosophy was itself facing what Lyotard or Derrida might have called a Crisis of Nomination. Not only was the term losing whatever residual sense it retained, there was a question of whether it actually existed in the first place.

Sokal's parody is exquisite:

It has . . . become increasingly apparent that physical 'reality', no less than social 'reality', is at bottom a social and linguistic construct; that scientific 'knowledge', far from being objective, reflects and encodes the dominant ideologies and power relations of the culture that produced it; that the truth claims of science are inherently theory-laden and self-referential; and consequently, that the discourse of the scientific community, for all its undeniable value, cannot assert a privileged epistemological status with

respect to counter-hegemonic narratives emanating from dissident or marginalized communities. These themes can be traced, despite some differences of emphasis, in Aronowitz's analysis of the cultural fabric that produced quantum mechanics; in Ross' discussion of oppositional discourses in post-quantum science; in Irigaray's and Hayles' exegeses of gender encoding in fluid mechanics; and in Harding's comprehensive critique of the gender ideology underlying the natural sciences in general and physics in particular.

And then when the novelist Laurent Binet published *The Seventh Function of Language* in 2017, a lucid and knowing fable about the pretensions, vanities, foibles and bizarre sexual preferences of Paris *intellos*, the Structuralist and Deconstructionist versions of the avant-garde became publicly risible. The rearguard had caught up and overtaken the vanguard. Here was a *dégringolade* of big egos and lofty reputations. And when they had fallen down the stairs of history, they were left in a disreputable heap.

Fine art, if that is what the Turner Prize represents, offers another example of how the avant-garde contains, as Marx might have said, the conditions of its own decline.

So much of the history of modern art has been based on 'revolutionary' assumptions. Picasso's *Demoiselles d'Avignon*, his 1907 masterpiece of early cubism, is routinely cited as such a revolution, with the Provençal hookers presented in astonishing pictorial fragments. Certainly Picasso, an accomplished thief of fire, took his inspiration where he could, and in this case from African masks. But it would be difficult to explain the value of this particular revolution to, say, a Choctaw Native American. But the same could be said for Impressionism.

Intended as an incubator of creativity, a shop window for novelty, the quintessence of the avant-garde, the Turner Prize has become fatuous and embarrassing. Proof, if proof were ever needed, that in the modern age artists have lost interest in beauty: at the Turner Prize, art has become a wearisome, joyless stunt. Its annual parade demonstrates that the avant-garde did not die. Nothing quite so exciting. It just became very boring. Few things are as dull as needy attempts to shock. Especially when they fail. Irrelevant too, except to a miniscule minority of cultists . . . people who possibly even believe an avant-garde exists.

A visit to an international art fair in Basel, Miami, London or Hong Kong shows that it does not. Everything is happening at once. The Frieze Art Fair in London now includes the once reviled 'Old Masters', acceptable now that they are in dollar terms cheaper than Jeff Koons's crapola. The great museums have become luxury brands: the Louvre Abu Dhabi is an aestheticised strip mall with a $450-million pseudo-Leonardo. Maybe there will be a British Museum Djakarta some time soon.

Meanwhile, Primo Levi insisted that after the Holocaust, poetry was impossible. And the evidence shows he was not entirely mistaken. Poetry today is a specialised, minority taste. And for anyone wanting nostalgically to replicate the olden-days shock value of the avant-garde, when painting prostitutes to look like Ibo masks guaranteed fame, 9/11 is a daunting precedent. The composer Karlheinz Stockhausen described it as 'Satan's greatest work of art'. Presence of true gods, or devils, is a good test for art.

There is no absolute logic to progress in thought or art. In a globalised world where Western values are not as absolute as once was thought, 'avant-garde' is meaningless. *Avant* to exactly what? And when the next-new-thing is discredited, what happens tomorrow?

Only history will know. And we are not history yet.

The Book
of Revelation

Napoli

▶ **Creativity can often be achieved by taking a very obvious message and expressing it in a very unobvious way.**

The city of Naples wanted to show that the buildings of Naples were crumbling, in order to raise money to restore them. They asked designer John McConnell to create a poster to make the point.

Instead of the obvious route of showing bits falling off the buildings, John spelt out the name of the city in elegant typography, and showed bits falling off the letters.

The decay of the city's name becomes a brilliant metaphor for the decay of the city itself.

A poster commissioned by
NAPOLI 99 Foundation as a contribution
towards the cultural image of the city

Brainstorming: a benefit to the hotel industry, but not to you or me

We've all been there: an early morning drive to a country house hotel somewhere in the Home Counties, the meeting-room table covered by a green baize cloth, set with ten places, each marked by a neat pad and pencil, an unnecessarily large supply of mineral water, a machine on the sideboard which dispenses stewed coffee and tepid tea in nine different flavours, and the flip chart on an easel in the corner waiting to record our spontaneous genius.

Yes, it's the awayday, one of the great arcane rituals of corporate life. The awayday, often called a brainstorm (an odd title, as there is no storm involved, and little brain), is corporate man's concession to creativity. The idea is to take a group of people who spend their working lives trapped in the discipline of rigid and risk-averse business thinking and liberate them to think freely, to create new answers. The Finance Director can be Fellini for a day; the Marketing Manager can be Manet for a day.

The goal of the brainstorm is to generate truly original thinking. And who could argue with such a fine ambition? Original thinking is at the very heart of creativity. But the problem doesn't lie with the ambition; it lies with the route to get to it.

Brainstorm days are, of course, hugely beneficial to the hotel industry. There's meeting-room hire, lunch for ten, a few overnight stays, with dinner, and it's all midweek when country house hotels are half empty. Most of those Cotswold hotels with Jaguars and BMWs parked on gravel drives would be bankrupt without brainstorms. But beneficial as they may be to hoteliers, they are of no use to anyone else.

The reason that the brainstorm doesn't work is that the idea is rooted in a fundamental misconception: the notion that group activity somehow equates with creative activity. The assumption is that if we all sit down together, throwing lots of ideas around, surely we'll come up with something?

No, we won't. Lateral thinking doesn't work like that.

The group dynamic of a brainstorm means that the responsibility for solving the problem is shared equally across the group, so there is no single person who has to do it. But lateral thinking is hard: it doesn't happen without the pressure of having to perform, of having to meet a deadline. And if the pressure is shared, the pressure is reduced.

There's a technical term for this phenomenon: it's called the Ringelmann effect, named after the French engineer who first observed it. His research showed that the larger the number in a group assigned to a task, the lower the productivity per head.

By contrast, someone who has to produce a creative answer on their own will be motivated not just by desire for success, but by fear of failure. I don't want to tell the outside world that I can't answer this problem, so I'll work ferociously to get an answer. But in a group, the sense of failure is diluted across the group. Indeed the failure is often not even recognised. At the end of a brainstorm, the participants kid themselves that they have solved the problem, even though they haven't. They congratulate each other – phrases like 'well done, very productive day . . .' ring out across the car park at six o'clock. People in a group tend to reinforce each other, creating the consensual illusion of a good result, when in truth that has not been achieved.

Ask yourself: How many of these days have you attended which subsequently led to a real business breakthrough?

No, me neither.

A second false assumption behind these awaydays is that we can change our mindset overnight. We've been cautious, thoughtful business people all our working lives – and suddenly, just because we're sitting in this agreeable hotel in Stow-on-the-Wold, we're instantly transformed into mad, idea-hungry, risk-taking creatives. It's just not realistic. You wouldn't expect to win Wimbledon if you hadn't picked up a tennis racket for half a year. To perform well, you need to be match fit, and that applies to the brain as well as the body.

The larger a corporation is, the more it has to lose. So all corporations tend to be cautious, and large corporations tend to be very cautious. Employees inevitably end up worrying less about how good their performance really is, and more about how good their performance looks to their boss. That makes for caution too. You can't change that for a day. Getting a big company to adopt a mindset which is imaginative, open-minded and entrepreneurial is a huge – though very necessary – task. Going off in a group for a day is barely scratching the surface of the problem.

It can even make the problem worse. In theory, when you all meet up for one of these day-long sessions, you're a team. But what makes a team in sport work together is the shared desire to beat the opposing team. Your team on a brainstorm day doesn't have any opposition: there is no enemy to unite against. So what happens? People who can't compete with an enemy (because there isn't one) compete with each other. The more aggressive members of the team start to score points, to show off. This undermines the group dynamic and it becomes a conflict of egos, not a conflation of ideas.

Sadly, a brainstorm is no more than a committee in nicer surroundings. And we all know that committees are not the natural habitat of creativity.

Did you ever see a statue of a committee?

A postscript: my co-author, Stephen, tells me that he has seen a statue of a committee. It's called *The Burghers of Calais* by Rodin – but it's round the corner from Victoria Station, so I rest my case.

Looking out,
looking in

When a woman has a baby, the process leading up to this magical moment comes in two clearly defined but very different stages: conception and gestation. Conception is, of course, a shared experience, whereas gestation is a personal journey. And while gestation takes nine months, conception might only take nine minutes. (I agree; it depends on how lucky you are in your choice of lover.)

It's not a bad metaphor for how an idea is born. That's also a two-stage process: first, the seed is sown, and then it develops into an idea with a life of its own. But – as with pregnancy – these two stages are fundamentally different in character.

The first stage is one of looking out at the rest of the world, to see where inspiration might lie. The second stage is the opposite: it's one where the artist looks inside him- or herself to uncover how that inspiration can be grown into a work of art.

The first stage is one of unending curiosity. Artists love talking to each other and looking at each other's work. The surrealists were so busy discussing and debating each other's work and philosophy, it's a wonder that they actually got any painting done themselves. It's not just a curiosity about other artists of the time: there's also a fascination with the artists of the past. Jake and Dinos Chapman, two of the more controversial of the Young British Artists, are obsessed with the art of Goya, and have used his etchings in their own work.

David Hockney is an unqualified fan of Picasso, and has often woven the great Spaniard's ideas into his own paintings and photography.

This fascination with other artists extends into different media. Painters soak up opera and theatre with the same enthusiasm that writers steep themselves in cinema or music. People with a creative gift are sponges for every form of creative expression.

The genesis of any great creative thought usually comes from the world outside: and since the work of other artists is a vivid window into that wider world, it is no surprise that creative minds love to steep themselves in the ideas of other creative minds.

But once the germ of an idea has been stimulated, the creative process leaps from the outer world to the inner world of the artist's own imagination. Creative ideas have to grow in solitude: they must be incubated in the privacy of the artist's soul. In a recent talk, the poet and novelist Ben Okri spoke sensitively about his 'room' where he developed ideas. But this was not a real room, in a real building: it was a compartment of his own mind, which he isolated from outside influence, the better to grow his ideas. It was his own private and solitary space, imagined yet utterly real, where he locked himself away to gestate his thoughts.

People who are not instinctively creative themselves like to think that ideas can come out of a group working together. But in that environment, the train of thought is inevitably logical: one suggestion leads to the next. That is a denial of true creativity, which depends on an utterly illogical creative leap.

This leap, this light-bulb moment, can usually only happen in solitude. It's true that in some areas of creativity a collaboration between two can work well. Ad agency creatives like to work in pairs, usually where one has a stronger verbal gift and the other has a stronger visual gift. And many of the great musicals were created by two-man teams: Rodgers and Hammerstein gave us great hits like

South Pacific and *The Sound of Music*, while more recently Tim Rice and Andrew Lloyd Webber gave us *Jesus Christ Superstar* and *Evita*. A form which involves words and music working together almost inevitably needs collaboration. But in every other art form, the idea emerges from a kind of solitary confinement. Even if, as in Ben Okri's case, that solitary confinement is itself a creation of the imagination.

Leave me alone!

▶ **Leave me alone! might be the most profound statement of creative intent.**

Petrarch was the first person to climb a mountain for intellectual recreation. His ambition was to 'avoid the tumult of cities' and avoid 'the thresholds of the proud'. Climbing Mont Ventoux and wandering the woods of the Vaucluse put him in a benign condition halfway between happiness and sadness, at least according to Ernest H. Wilkins in *Petrarch at Vaucluse* (1958).

In a letter of 1783, Mozart said that his thoughts prospered best when he was entirely alone and in a good mood. The circumstances might be while travelling in a carriage between Vienna and Prague, ambling around after a good dinner or even in a sleeplessly restless *nuit blanche*. He did not know where his ideas came from – they seemed automatic and beyond the reach of will – but what was certain was that the idea, once identified, enlarged and defined itself, and this process took place in a 'pleasing, lively dream'. Then, in his original German: '*Gleich alles zusammen!*' Or, 'Everything comes together!'

Privacy is about personal identity, sex, hygiene, manners, architectural space, human rights, religious contemplation and creative solitude. It is extremely precious, but it is under threat.

Our notion of privacy is an invention of recent history, not much older than the steam engine. Its creation is intimately involved with the evolving modern idea of 'personality', the belief that each of us has distinctive traits, that our 'self' has a secret formula. But privacy is not the same as mere secrecy. Privacy includes ideas about personal freedom and the organisation of culture.

Privacy did not exist in the historic past and, as the internet, social media, metadata, hacking and CCTV surveillance threaten to make intimacy public, privacy may not exist in future.

When the traveller Sir Richard Burton found Arab women bathing naked in an oasis, they spontaneously covered their faces when they realised they were being observed by European men. Their religion taught them that the face was more a 'private part' than the sexual organs.

When the traveller Sir Richard Burton found Arab women bathing naked in an oasis, they spontaneously covered their faces when they realised they were being observed by European men. Their religion taught them that the face was more a 'private part' than the sexual organs. In the European Middle Ages, eating, bathing and sleeping were communal. It was only in the nineteenth century that a woman might bathe without attendants. We are (still) successors to that assumption . . . but only just.

Western notions of cultivated life have all tended to nurture ideas about privacy: the monk in his cell, the artist in his atelier, the *hortus conclusus*, Thoreau in his hut on Walden Pond. Proust's work is full of references to the creative benefits of solitude. As Patrick Leigh Fermor explained in *A Time to Keep Silence* (1957), the monastic retreat is the best remedy for urban anxiety. In domestic architecture, we value the interplay between shared space and personal space. Few would want to live in a house with no privacy.

Privacy is even protected by the UN Universal Declaration of Human Rights, a forensic idea that can be traced back to the *Harvard Law Review* of 1890 in an article by Samuel D. Warren and Louis Brandeis called 'The Right to Privacy'. When our privacy is threatened, so too is our freedom, yet so many of the pressures in contemporary life conspire to reduce the individual's access to privacy. A person who cultivates privacy sets himself apart from the controlling forces of contemporary life. Thus, advocating privacy is a privilege that is contrary to the accepted order. Thus, creative in spirit.

And our ideas about privacy are culturally determined. There is no exact Italian equivalent and Russian uses a word semantically halfway between 'secrecy' and 'private life'. Our contemporary notion of 'privacy' is essentially Anglo-American, an expression of our concerns and preoccupations and our culture's megalomania. Private dining, private medicine and private banking are ways of defining our unique personalities.

That we value privacy so highly is indicated by the fact that medical records and voting histories are fiercely protected by law and most of us would prefer our intimate activities to be our own, not the public's. And intrusions into privacy are often illegal. 'Private parts' suggests the ultimate intimacy with oneself and others.

Are privacy and solitude the crucibles of thought? Certainly, a crowded tube or the journey between Junctions 17 and 18 of the M4 does not encourage calm reflection. But the idea of the lonely artist is historically specific: it is one of the many cultural products of the Renaissance. The patron Isabella d'Este, for example, spoke of the *bizzarria* of artists: their almost wilful oddness and antisociability.

Niccolo dell'Arca, sculptor, creator of the largest terracottas in the world, the *Compianto sul Cristo Morto* in Bologna's Santa Maria della

Vita, was said by a contemporary chronicler, Girolamo Borselli, to have repulsive and barbaric manners, no pupils and no friends. Piero di Cosimo, to choose just one more example from a rich tradition of solitary eccentricity, routinely dined alone on up to fifty boiled eggs. Even the Divine Michelangelo was outside polite society, ruled by *gran passione*, a great distress that, late in life, made him suspect he was going mad.

But there are contrary forces: crowd-sourcing is now promoted above creative solitude. The internet wants to find out everything about you. And it can. Maybe 'privacy' was only a passing moment . . . just like the steam engine. Maybe in future everything will be explicit and shared. Then again, maybe not.

But best to appreciate solitude and protect privacy. Then again, if solitude were more generous a muse then perhaps hermits and prisoners on punishment regimes might be more creative.

Skunkworks

For every argument in favour of privacy and solitude, there is a counter-argument about how very effective it can be to work in organised groups. Artists are not always sociopaths shivering in unheated studios, communing with muses and having a tragic tussle with destiny and the bottle. Raphael and Rubens were rich men, socialites who ran big, prosperous studios with managers and assistants. They knew how to delegate, not to abnegate.

Then there is the phenomenon of the artists' colony. That the concept appeals so strongly to the collective element in the German mentality is revealed by the existence of a unique word to describe them: *Künstlerdorf*. Sometimes creativity thrives in communes with shared values. Barbizon, Roycroft, Le Pouldu, Pont-Aven, Worpswede and St Ives are just the most well-known examples. Often, exceptionally beautiful surroundings prove stimulating. At Worpswede, the poet Rilke was a guest and he found: 'There is a sky of indescribable variations and magnitude begins.'

And writers also have their retreats at, for instance, Yaddo in Saratoga Springs (although it might be admitted that writers' retreats are not always encouraging to genius or productive of masterpieces since generous grants and comfortable residential accommodation are not always stimulating).

True, van Gogh and Matisse worked alone, the former in very

trying circumstances with absinthe and self-harm, but, by contrast, Andy Warhol called his studio the Factory to indicate his infatuation with the twentieth century as well as the industrial processes used

by the large population of collaborator-workers (and transvestites) therein. Damien Hirst often has no physical contact with the works of art his very many people manufacture for him.

Besides, the defining art forms of the twentieth century are collaborative ones. The movies, rock music and industrial design do not have individual 'auteurs', but entire teams of technicians and artists working together. Who is the creative source of a film? The writer? Director? Cinematographer? The sound stage at Warner Brothers was not a place of privacy or solitude. Nor was the Writers' Room.

Designers especially like to create stimulating environments: when his team was working on the astonishing Studebaker Avanti, for reasons of secrecy, esprit du corps and PR (science cannot determine the priority here), Raymond Loewy insisted they were locked into his Albert Frey-designed house at 600 W Panorama Road in Palm

'It's not rocket science' is, surely, one of the most annoying expressions in contemporary life.

Springs. And they were not let out until the design had been finalised. In Santa Monica, the Eames House was not just a residence for Charles and Ray, but an academy with master and disciples. California seems especially propitious to creative colonies: movies and rock music have an almost religious status here.

And so too does aerospace. Lockheed's 'Skunk Works' in Burbank was one of the most brilliant artists' colonies ever. 'It's not rocket science' is, surely, one of the most annoying expressions in contemporary life. Although it is some comfort to know its source. This is probably a sports article in the *Philadelphia Daily Intelligencer* published in 1985. It says: 'Coaching football is not rocket science and it's not brain surgery. It's a game, nothing more.' Anyway, it was a creative coinage: memorability may be a test for the presence of the true creative spirit.

So we know what rocket science is not. Rocket science is not commonplace, ordinary stuff. It's not the obvious. Rocket science is clever. (As a matter of fact, rocket science is a fusion of fluid dynamics, astrophysics, statics, mathematics, electronics, propulsion technology, control systems, structures, materials science, risk analysis.)

The Skunk Works was not rocket science; it was more. The name comes from the moonshine factory of Dogpatch, Kentucky, in Al Capp's hillbilly cartoon *Li'l Abner*, which was a United Features Syndicate running for forty-three years until 1977. In Dogpatch, lethal fumes from the distillery killed many residents each year. In Burbank, a malodorous plastic factory inspired the happy nomination.

Lockheed's Skunk Works had its origins in 1938 when a small group of engineers was sequestered, segregated and, quite literally, walled off. They were working on a project called XP-38, which became known as the Lockheed P-38 (or 'Lightning' to the RAF). This was the most advanced piston-engined plane ever: a completely original concept. It would not be true to say that it exceeded every contract requirement, because at the Skunk Works there never were any contracts. Major military commissions proceeded on a handshake with no official procurement procedures.

The presiding genius at the Skunk Works was Clarence L. Johnson, always known as 'Kelly', who had won a prize for aircraft design when he was just thirteen. His watchwords were: 'Be quick, be quiet, be on time.' When in 1943 they needed a design to exploit the British Goblin engine (at the time the US was behind in jet technology), it took Kelly Johnson's team just a month to present the XP-80 proposal. And it took a mere 143 further days to create the actual plane. This was the famous Lockheed Shooting Star.

Equally fabulous machinery followed from the Skunk Works:

the U-2 spy plane and the SR-71 'Blackbird' ram-jet, which can travel from Los Angeles to London in 3 hours, 47 minutes and 39 seconds (including two periods of slowing down for in-flight refuelling). More recent Skunk Works projects have included the F-117 Nighthawk, F-22 Raptor and F-35 Lighting II. Plus, there can be no doubt, a very great number of other projects which are not our business.

Besides extreme vision, a taste for secrecy and subterfuge was a part of the Skunk Works method: when, for example, Lockheed needed aircraft-grade titanium, a dummy corporation was set up to source it from the Soviet Union. Kelly Johnson was not only an aerospace designer of incomparable originality, he was also an organisational genius who knew about creative teamwork.

And he had his own Rules of Management:

Give managers autonomy.
A small number of good people is better than a large number of mediocre people.

Don't waste time writing reports.
Tolerate change, but anticipate problems
(especially financial ones).
Trust people and reward them generously.
Don't work in solitude, but keep projects private.

At the Skunk Works, there was a creative culture that prevented a regression to the mean that inevitably occurs when too many people are involved. Small, diverse teams steal fire better than large, homogenous ones. They also make rocket science appear dull.

A little learning is a dangerous thing – too much learning can be worse

▶ **It's widely assumed that Isaac Newton discovered gravity when he saw an apple fall from a tree. It's also quite wrong: the truth is very different, and it's very startling.**

What really triggered Newton's insight was a violent and tragic epidemic. The Great Plague, as it was known, broke out in and around London in 1665. The disease was caused by a bacterium carried by fleas on rats. Its effects were devastating. In London, more than 100,000 people died: nearly a quarter of the city's total population at that time.

Newton had been working close to London, at Cambridge University. There he was surrounded by wonderful libraries where he could study, and other brilliant academics with whom he could debate ideas. For these intellectuals, observing the phenomenon of gravity was hardly new: any fool could see that if you held something and then let go, it would fall to the ground. The big scientific question was: Why? But while the question was easy to define, it proved astonishingly hard to answer. Newton struggled.

Then the plague hit. It was not only lethal, it was also highly contagious. Like many others, Newton quarantined himself. He took refuge in his own house, and did not emerge for two years, so fearful was he of contracting the killer disease. During that time he was in self-imposed exile from books and libraries, and from other thinkers. He had nothing to fill his mind.

And that was when his theory of gravitation started to form – not when his brain was filled with information, but when it was empty.

We are all educated to think that the more we learn, the more information we have, the more data we analyse, then the better equipped we will be to solve a problem. It's certainly true that understanding a problem in depth puts us in a good place to reach for a solution. But when we have fully understood the problem and need to move to a creative answer, too much information can only get in the way. The creative process demands a clear head, not an over-filled one.

It's sobering to observe the world of modern politics. The politician of today has any amount of information at his disposal: focus groups, economic data, opinion polls. Yet public respect for politicians has never been more grudging. It's clear that they understand the problems they face. But it's also clear that they seem paralysed when it comes to doing anything to attack those problems. Information overload has stifled any spontaneity and imagination.

In taking the step from understanding to solution, you are taking a step from a world where information is crucial to one where imagination is crucial. At the understanding stage, the more you know the better: but at the solution stage what is needed is an open mind, not a full one.

That's why creative people often prefer to work in a place of solitude. They want to be in a space where their mind can wander entirely unconstrained. Too much information tells you what you can't do more eloquently than it tells you what you can do. A blank sheet of paper and a pencil is much more inspiring than a lever-arch file crammed with statistics.

If you want the creative ideas to flow, don't spend too long learning stuff: try to unlearn instead. Empty your mind, so there is room for new inspiration to find its way in.

It's worth thinking what we mean by 'creativity'. Really, we mean the ability to think of new ideas, ideas which haven't been considered before. By definition, something which is innovative is unlike what exists now. So too much knowledge about the world as it is can often get in the way of imagining the world as it could be.

Too much information tells you what you can't do more eloquently than it tells you what you can do.

Education: a curse on creativity

▶ **We like to think that education is building the future of our society. We struggle to get our children into good schools. We push them and encourage them while they are there. Their every small success is a reason for a celebration, while their every small failure precipitates another outburst of parental anxiety. When they achieve good enough grades to get into university, we sigh with the relief that comes from knowing that their future is secure.**

How nice it would be if this value system actually worked. But it doesn't.

We can readily observe that getting to a good university no longer guarantees a stable career. (Did it ever?) We can observe that people who become high achievers in life were often disasters at school. There is clear evidence that a disproportionately high percentage of successful entrepreneurs did not even complete their schooling, let alone excel at it. We see that those who leave school as Head Boy or Head Girl surprisingly often end up as Head-of-nothing-very-much. Research indicates that school success does not necessarily lead to career success: often the reverse is true. And research also shows that failure at school does not necessarily lead to career failure: again, the opposite is often true.

In short, we all believe that our great education is paving the way to our great career – even though the evidence shows that this is nonsense. What is going on?

The answer is depressing, but simple. There are many different ways of being clever, but conventional schools only recognise one of them.

Let's explore this a bit: what exactly do I mean when I say that 'there are many different ways of being clever'? Well, we are all familiar with the concept of emotional intelligence: it's the kind of intelligence which helps us relate to people, as opposed to the conventional type of intelligence which is more to do with how we relate to intellectual, rather than human, issues. Emotional intelligence matters, because in life it's no use having the right answer if you can't get other people to buy into that right answer.

Some people have high intelligence in analysing a problem, but lack the imaginative gift to solve it. Some people have a high imaginative intelligence, so they can find the answer to a problem. But you need a different type of cleverness – one which is long on detail and diligence – to get that solution put into practice effectively.

We see it all the time in our everyday lives: some people are good at communicating, some are good at solving, some are good at inventing, some are good at persisting to see things through and to make sure the good idea actually gets delivered. We need all of these skills. A good team is simply a grouping of different ways of being clever. If you were a football manager, you wouldn't keep the job long (even by football-manager standards) if you fielded a team of eleven goalkeepers. Eleven centre forwards wouldn't do that well either.

It's not a complicated idea to grasp. Yet schools don't grasp it. Look at the syllabus for any normal school, and look at the way that school is run. You will see, not just in Britain but throughout the world, that mathematics and language are privileged above all other subjects. Scientific subjects follow closely. The arts are at the bottom of the heap, almost regarded as an inconvenience.

Sporting achievement is also valued. (I always assumed at my school that the masters focused the teenage boys on sport in the vain hope that it would take their minds off girls.) But even in sport, there is a hierarchy: team games like rugby or football are much more valued than individual sports like tennis or golf.

What messages does this system send to our children?

First, it tells them that analytical and logical thought is to be valued very much more highly than creative and imaginative thought.

Second, it tells them that individual activity is of lesser significance than team activity. And, of course, we see in other chapters of this book that creativity is, at its heart, an individual activity; and a team dynamic often stifles rather than stimulates new thinking.

In short, we're teaching our children that creativity and inventiveness aren't that important – and if you have any kind of creative gift, you're not very important either, thank you very much.

It gets worse than that. That's because our teaching system, focused on only one type of cleverness, teaches us that there is a right answer – and only one – to a question. For instance, although we can see that at university level mathematics starts to become creative, the maths questions we normally face at school have just one correct answer. The meta-language of this is alarming: if there is only one answer, fresh thinking is unnecessary, even unhelpful.

> **We're teaching our children that creativity and inventiveness aren't that important – and if you have any kind of creative gift, you're not very important either.**

The whole essence of creative thinking is that there is always another different, potentially better, way of looking at things. Our education system is a living denial of this truth. That's because the subjects like mathematics which are susceptible to the 'there is one right answer' analysis are at the top of the educational status tree. Whereas the subjects like art which offer the possibility of end-less new answers are at the very bottom of that status tree.

Underlying all this is a belief that the purpose of schooling is to help you get a good job. (And I thought that schooling was to help you become a thoughtful, curious and intelligent human being – and with those assets, you'd be able to get a good job anyway. Silly me.)

Education has become a means to a very specific end: learn how to pass this exam, learn how to get to university, learn how to get a job as a lawyer. But actually education only has real meaning when it's an end in itself: learn how to become more enquiring, more inventive, more developed as a human being.

The tyranny of education over imagination is much worse in schools where the parents pay. We like to think, as we cash our life savings to put our little ones into private schooling, that we are doing the best for them.

If only.

The truth is that the dynamic changes, in a most unhealthy way, when the school is funded by the parent, not the government. The focus is no longer on the child but on the parent, because it's the parent who is the paying customer. So if Daddy, who's a partner in a big accountancy firm, wants young Rupert to follow in his footsteps, he doesn't want to hear how well Rupert is doing in drama. He wants to hear that Rupert got full marks in his maths homework. Which is why Rupert ends up as an unfulfilled accountant instead of an accomplished theatre producer.

If you believe that creativity is a vibrant and crucial strand in the human spirit (and if you don't, you've made a bad mistake in buying this book), then my concerns about education are worth pondering. To be clear, I have no quarrel with teachers: they are usually selfless people, intelligent and kind, who give very long hours for very little money. And even less thanks. No, my quarrel is with the bad system in which these good people are made to work. It's a system which acts as a curse on our creativity, eating it away from within.

It teaches that creative activities are inferior to analytical activities. It teaches that it is unnecessary, wrong even, to look for a new solution. It teaches that individual brilliance is not to be trusted: it's only the team that counts. And it teaches you that your purpose in life is to achieve employment, not fulfilment.

Is that what we really want for our children and our future?

RM

Four white men

▶ **A while ago I wrote a book called** *The Rule Breaker's Book of Business*. **It was about thinking more laterally, more imaginatively in business. I was then asked to do some talks about it, and that led to invitations to advise businesses on how they could be more innovative.**

One of these companies asked me to their head office in London; they said that one of them had seen my presentation and enjoyed it, and had then shared the book with some of their colleagues. They were desperate to introduce new ideas to their company, to learn how to think differently. Could I help?

There were four of them in the meeting: all courteous and intelligent businessmen, but struggling with the burdensome question of how to be a bit different. I looked at them, and found it hard to suppress a smile.

Eventually, I plucked up the courage to say what I was thinking.

'Look,' I said. 'There are four of you briefing me. You say that you all want to think differently. But you are all white, all middle class, all male, all well educated. You probably even play golf at the same club. When you talk to each other, you'll inevitably tend to get similar views because you come from similar backgrounds. If you want to have different thoughts, it would help if you employed different sorts of people.'

I didn't get the job.

Sometimes, the truth hurts too much. But I think my observation was right. Similar types of people tend to reinforce each other; but if you want to think differently you don't need reinforcement, you need challenge.

Companies who are eager to hire bright women as well as bright men, to hire good people from all kinds of social and ethnic backgrounds, will be much better equipped to think differently – because they are themselves different from each other.

It's currently fashionable for businesses to pursue more diversity in the people they hire. That's done because it looks good in the annual report: it shows the business is run by caring people. But there is a much more compelling, commercial reason for diverse hiring: a diverse staff brings a range of different ideas and attitudes to a problem. Which means an imaginative answer is far more likely.

'If you want to have different thoughts, it would help if you employed different sorts of people.'

There is no better example of the dangers of reinforcement than those tragicomic annual events, the conferences of the big political parties. Here the Tory leadership address the Tory faithful; or the Labour leadership address the Labour activists. In either case, there is much preaching to the converted and little else. The idea is to send the party supporters home with a buoyant feeling that everything is OK. Trouble is, it's usual in politics that everything isn't OK: there are real problems to be resolved.

A party political conference is a mechanism to talk about problems with people who already share your view – so it's pretty much guaranteed that no original thinking will take place.

If you want to think differently, you need to seek out those who have a different perspective from you. If you tend to be conservative, get advice from someone who's radical. If you are risk-averse, talk to someone who's an entrepreneur.

It's easier to say that than to do it, because instinctively we all tend to gang up with 'people like us'. But if you are going to get to an innovative resolution to a problem, you have to bite the bullet: get views from those who challenge and question, not those who reinforce.

Thinking outside the box: lazy clichés

▶ The artistic merits of John Cage's silent piece of music, *4'33"*, will be debated forever, or, perhaps, never. But it is certain that Cage had no exaggerated respect for the rules. In an audience's expectations he saw little to respect. He wrote:

> **the past must be Invented**
> **the future Must be**
> **revIsed . . .**

Cage was not in a box.

A box is a container of known dimensions and determined size. Pandora's may have contained unwelcome surprises, but – in general – boxes are not remarkable.

Boxes are usually symmetrical and their corners are mostly right angles: ninety degrees is a pusillanimous compromise between veering left or veering right. It is neither. It is the middle way. Thus, to be despised. The middle way never got anybody anywhere. Turn around the middle way and you are back where you started from.

Ninety degrees is only 'right' in that it cannot possibly be wrong. It is boring. Additionally, boxes can be stacked in orderly ways even unto infinity to create a Hades of uniformity. Boxes are not very exciting. Coffins are an exception. These are boxes of irregular shape whose

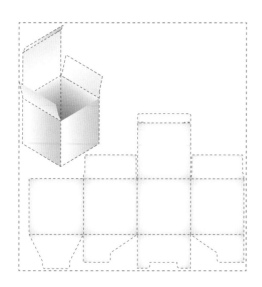

purpose is to accommodate expired vitality. To be sure, boxes are deadly dull: predictable, constraining, ordinary, reminiscent of death.

So an invitation to 'think outside the box' is an invitation to be daring and unconventional. It is an expression often used by motivational speakers, management consultants, people who go to conferences in lanyards or any lazy know-all who mistakes a weary trope for provocation.

In this expression, a box is a metaphor of constraint, but over-used metaphors become clichés and clichés are never interesting. Even articulating the expression 'think outside the box' shows you are a slave to conventionality and easy-thinking. Creative people never think outside the box because creative people don't even recognise the existence of a constraining box in the first place. To think outside the box accepts that known borders exist. To creative people, they do not.

It was the dismayingly conventional Walt Disney Company that coined the 'thinking outside of the box' trope. The reference was the famous nine-dot puzzle where a 3×3 matrix was the 'box'. In management training the task was to connect the dots without lifting pen off paper or retracing any part of the line you have drawn. It's easily done in four simple strokes if you look beyond the obvious and see a larger pattern. People who solve the nine-dot puzzle actually *see* a different pattern, a better opportunity. They are not constrained.

But acknowledging that a box exists, even if to step outside it, betrays you as a conventional thinker stuck on precedent. After all, the Magic Kingdom is over sixty years old. Just ask the Creative

Thinking Association of America, which is still keen on 3×3 matrices. Yawn.

If we accepted that boxes existed, an example would be saying something in favour of bad behaviour. Or 'steal like an artist'.

The poet Jean Lorrain thought 'a bad reputation never did anyone any harm'. It is really quite hard to prove that unblemished virtue is an asset to a business. Indeed, it is easy to make the opposite case. Perhaps not all the seven deadly sins are useful in management: sloth, for example, is no one's friend, but avarice and lust are terrific motivators.

Meanwhile, no one is going to publish a book called *Seven Saintly Stratagems to Protect Your Bottom Line* because it would be very boring and would not sell, but *Unscrupulous Advice from the Very Rich* would surely be an attractive title. And a thicker volume than the other one.

Hunter S. Thompson once said that, looking around at his friends and colleagues, indeed, looking at himself, and considering how very happy and successful everyone was, he would positively recommend committed, long-term abuse of drugs and alcohol. It is the same with sin in business. We may need more of it.

I am not talking about vulgar criminals, although common criminals and business visionaries share certain traits: they have huge egos and see a system that is vulnerable to exploitation for personal gain. Of course, criminality is not attractive, although remember that Bernard Madoff had many admirers and investors until the very end. Like the German intellectuals with the Nazis, a great many otherwise sensible people found him entirely plausible.

Instead, there is a more subtle case to be made for the place of wickedness in business. And this case has historical credentials so profound that it is tempting to argue a general theory that business is amoral and that a record of social conscience or good behaviour or polite deference or well-maintained scruples do not necessarily make any contribution to success. They might even militate against it.

Any survey of sin's place in good management must begin with Cesare Borgia, the illegitimate son of a pope and one of the great soldiers and statesmen and corrupters and murderers of the Renaissance. Borgia existed in a stew of universal depravity where incest, back-stabbing, front-stabbing and poisoning were routine. He was the inspiration for Niccolò Machiavelli's *The Prince*. This was the first how-to book and Machiavelli was the prototype management consultant. His top tip was, and I paraphrase, the ends justify the means: decide what you want and go for it.

The men whose iron, coal and railroads made industrial America possible were called 'Robber Barons', not 'Civic-Minded Philanthropists'. Theft is a common theme in success. Picasso, we have heard, knew that truly great artists don't borrow, they steal. Between inspiration and theft there is a line so fine it is nearly invisible. Anyway, true creativity may just be knowing how to disguise your sources.

Henry Ford used armed thugs to break strikes and was a virulent anti-Semite. During the Second World War, Mercedes-Benz and BMW 'employed' slave labour to manufacture war materiel. Ferdinand Porsche mumbled he was just-doing-his-job when he put his design consultancy in the service of Hitler, creating Panzer tanks and supervising the manufacture of the V-1 buzz bomb. The war encouraged business duplicity: after 1945 the old US ITT conglomerate claimed compensation for damage caused by Allied bombing of the Focke-Wulf factories it owned. Good business, but poor scruples.

Suspicion that it subverts governments and certainty that it sells destructive obesity products have not stopped Coca-Cola becoming the world's biggest beverage business. Steve Jobs was a borderline psychotic and a bully. Many believe that Richard Branson's richly deserved knighthood was delayed awaiting clarification about the legality of some early business activity. Bernie Ecclestone has only recently begun to talk openly about his long-alleged involvement with the Great Train Robbery. He denied it all, adding mischievously that there was not, in any case, enough money on the train to make the heist worthwhile in business terms. It's a matter of cost and benefit, you know.

The question is not so much about sin in business, but the more general one that many of life's activities discourage morality and encourage loutishness. For example, to make progress in traffic, good manners and foresight are actual handicaps. Traffic rewards brutality and stupidity. The meek do not inherit the fast lane.

Still, we admire success, even if we are often unhappy about the way it has been achieved. The moral mutability is revealed once in that wonderful line from the novelist Samuel Butler: 'I don't mind lying, but I detest inaccuracy.' And second in that marvellous line of Malcolm McLaren's about his technically inept fledgling band, the Sex Pistols: 'They are so bad, they are good.' There's a thought.

Too much No, No, not enough Yes, Yes

We like to think that education is all about learning what you can do: you can do algebra, you can do grammar, you can do French verbs, and so on. It's an appealing notion, but it's a misleading half-truth. Because much of what we're taught is not about what we can do, but about what we can't.

You can't cross the road without looking, you can't be rude to Grandma, you can't play with the gas hob. Admonitions like these are crucial to us as children because they aim to inculcate basic concepts of safety and courtesy. And because they're basic, they're taught very early on. If our education seems to offer too much of what we can't and not enough of what we can, that's particularly true when we're very young.

This guidance by prohibition is very necessary. If we weren't told as children not to put our hand in a flame, the consequences would be horrendous.

Yet this training comes at a price. It teaches us that the adult world is a place of inhibition and control. And one of the forces which becomes inhibited is our own imagination. Our minds become habituated to the idea that there are boundaries, which must be respected; that there's a correct way of doing something; that there are proprieties to be observed. If we want an ordered society, this education is valuable. But if we want new ideas, it's death.

Our freedom to think as we wish becomes buried deep inside us, often never to escape. To quote Nietzsche, 'In every real man a child is hidden that wants to play.'

Creativity thrives on doing things differently, on finding new paths. Respect for the current systems stifles new thinking. Ask a child to draw a dinosaur. They might paint it pink, because it's not a traditional dinosaur colour, but it's fun. They might give it wheels instead of legs, because . . . well, because why not? But ask an adult to draw a dinosaur and they'll do their clumsy best to draw something that conforms to our existing ideas of what dinosaurs looked like. In other words, the adult mind is educated to follow rules; the child is allowed to break them. Which is why most children have a creative sensitivity that adults lack. As Groucho Marx said when looking at a problem, 'A child of five would understand this. Send someone to fetch a child of five.'

Give a child a set of crayons on a plane trip, and they'll doodle ferociously for hours. Give an adult a set of crayons, and they'll look embarrassed before turning back to the *Financial Times*.

We are born with a natural gift for play and fantasy – two forces which are at the heart of creativity. But these gifts are drilled out of us as we grow up. That is why most adults find it deeply difficult to think creatively. The freedom to let our imagination run wild has been disciplined out of us. Picasso said: 'Every child is an artist. The problem is how to remain an artist once he grows up.'

It is also why creative personalities are often capable of being childish, selfish, even petulant. They can behave like children – because something in their make-up has survived all that teaching about what you can't do. They are still in a world of 'I can do what I want, I can imagine what I like'. That's necessary to feed their creativity, but it brings with it behaviour other adults would condemn as immature.

If you observe childlike behaviour in a creative person, forgive them. It's part of how they are. And if you want to be more creative in your own thinking, try to emulate a child's ability to imagine a world where there are no boundaries, where anything could happen.

Picasso (again) understood this well when he said:

'It took me four years to paint like Raphael, but a lifetime to paint like a child.'

The biggest risk of all

▶ **We know that to accomplish anything, we must first attempt it. And we know that our attempt may be met with success or failure. So an attempt to achieve could lead to failure. But we also know that if we don't make that attempt, failure is certain. Therefore, it must be better to make the attempt – that route offers the possibility of failure, while to do nothing offers the certainty of failure.**

The logic of this unchallengeable. Yet the reality is that while we embrace this concept intellectually, often we reject it emotionally. We find spurious reasons to justify our own inaction, even though we know that this denies us the opportunity of success.

We are, almost all of us, innately rather more risk-averse than is healthy.

Why are we so illogical, and so downright timid? There are, I believe, three forces at work.

The first is that the fear of failure looms larger in our mind than the hope of success. Human beings can't tolerate any kind of rejection, any more than camels can dance. The thought that our idea might be turned down stirs stronger emotions than the possibility it might not be.

Second, most humans have a bizarre lack of self-belief. We're just not a confident species. So we assume that failure is more likely than success. This, of course, becomes a self-fulfilling prophecy. Henry

Ford wisely said: 'Whether you think you can do it or you think you can't, you're probably right.'

Third, we like to kid ourselves that the status quo is healthier than it really is. Faced with the risk of setting out on a journey we may not complete, we tell ourselves that we're really very happy staying where we are. There is no need to move on, as we are in a good place now.

All of this constipated thinking kills creativity. The world of innovation, by definition, demands that we are willing to try something new. And that means taking a risk: something we are disproportionately terrified of.

If we are going to understand creative ideas, let alone have one ourselves, it's vital to climb out of this negative and complacent mindset. That's not easy. It's a bit like giving up smoking: we have to deploy a huge amount of willpower to escape from a habit we know is unhealthy, but we also know is a habit that makes us comfortable.

We see buildings like the Guggenheim in Bilbao, an extraordinary confection that has transformed the fortunes of a city, and we observe the success of entrepreneurs, whose energy not only makes a fortune for themselves but creates employment for others – but we don't join the dots. We know that these things don't happen unless people are willing to take risks: but we are still much too grudging about taking risks ourselves.

Put simply, we spend far too much time thinking about what might go wrong, and far too little time thinking about what might go right.

We need to remember that the biggest risk of all is never to take a risk.

We need to remember that the biggest risk of all is never to take a risk.

The bitch-goddess success

Most people dwell on success. Often morbidly. Here is the poet Robert Frost:

**No memory of having starred
Atones for later disregard
Or keeps the end from being hard.**

There are no better bittersweet words on the fragility of high achievement.

Most people crave the approbation of a Higher Authority who will, in the recurrent dream, tap them on the shoulder and say: 'Well done! You've made it!' But that never happens except in sinister cults, so most people find a crude surrogate in the acquisition of stuff or the acclaim of peers. But what happens if your new Porsche 911 GT3 does not have a transformative effect on your psychic hygiene? Success is elusive. Try embracing fog to get a sense of its intangibility.

Is success getting things right? Is failure getting things wrong?

It's really not as simple as that. People who steal fire find binary thinking crude and unsatisfactory. Fire stealers do not have conventional views, or, indeed, any views susceptible to numerical analysis or portion control. It's safe to say that portion control, a mimsy sliver of butter in foil or a fiddly sachet of industrial sauce, is a device that says as much about the meanness of the proprietor as the greed

of the consumer. A fire stealer would know that the generosity stratagem of saying 'Help yourself!' worked better than restricting people
to 25 mg of edible fats.

Fire stealers are damnably cussed: Mark Twain believed all you
needed to ensure (a version of) success was a winning mixture of
ignorance and confidence.

Anyway, success, Nietzsche said, is a 'liar'. A false god(dess). And it
follows that failure might reflect a terrible form of truth. Or maybe,
in a peculiar way, it is the other way around. If, that is, success and
failure are opposites rather than different parts of the same whole.

If success is owning two iPads, that Porsche or a top-of-the-range
Mercedes, a statement wristwatch and a home cinema, then it cannot
be very difficult or precious. And yet so much emotional and practical
effort is spent in pursuit of this delusion. If you Google 'success in
business', over three hundred million results are quickly shown, dispiriting evidence of frustrated global yearnings . . . most of them
dismayingly banal: 'show up, keep up, shut up' is one example. Or
John Paul Getty's 'rise early, work hard, strike oil' is another.

Although it is fair to caution that anyone needing Google for guidance in the matter of success probably lacks the elements of
personality and motivation essential to the achievement. Søren
Kierkegaard believed: 'The best demonstration of the misery of
existence is given by the contemplation of its marvels.' What misery
the accumulation of stuff suggests!

The grail of hard and shiny blemish-free arithmetical success was
a fixed point in twentieth-century business books and, indeed, in
twentieth-century business schools. This was mocked by that great
mocker Vance Packard in *The Pyramid Climbers* (1962) where 'execu-
tives' (now a nearly extinct subspecies of humanity) edged up the
ziggurat edge of the business pyramid, lodging on ever more altitu-
dinous ledges as they ascended.

Packard suspected the presence of a commanding goddess, both 'feather-headed and ruthless', at the summit. In this pyramid model, real success was rare and absolute: the nearer you got to the precarious top, the less space there was available. And room at the very pinnacle was restricted to a single individual. Thus the wretched CEO with his pension pot and his myopic horizons, his short-term vision and his short-term job.

We owe the splendid expression 'the bitch-goddess success' to William James, the Pragmatist and novelist Henry's brother. Many thought William the more creative individual, even if he were the less 'successful'. The expression 'stream of consciousness' is, for example, James's. And he founded the school of Pragmatism, which argued that a hypothesis is worth supporting if 'consequences useful to life flow from it'. If it's good for you, do it! Who would not want to be a Pragmatist?

The bitch-goddess source is a letter James wrote to his friend H. G. Wells in 1906: 'The moral flabbiness born of the exclusive worship of the bitch-goddess success that – with the squalid cash interpretation put on the word "success" – is our national disease,' he says. D. H. Lawrence picked up on this and popularised the expression. Success, Lawrence thought, tended to snarl. And snarling was not a good thing.

It's important to recognise that failure is not at all the same thing as being a loser. No one wants to be a loser, but the creative will be proud of his failures. The engaging paradox in the failure–success discussion is that failure is so much more interesting and stimulating. In failure, there is something noble and beautiful. Creative people have no fear of it. Indeed, they embrace it, even, that is, if they recognise it in the first place. James Joyce said: 'A man of genius makes no mistakes; his errors are volitional and are the portals of discovery.' Perhaps only losers really see events and activities as failures.

Creative people do a lot of stuff. Fire stealers are rarely idle and feckless, despite the luminous example of a forever prevaricating Leonardo. According to Vasari in *The Lives of the Artists* (1550, first English edition 1908), Leonardo was preposterously erratic in his work on *The Last Supper* in Milan: periods of intense concentration were punctuated by bewildering absences.

Perhaps he was reluctant to finish it. This continuous process of deferment is a part of the creative personality: to reach a conclusion too soon is to deny the dynamics of the process. Deadlines may be inimical to creativity because the best ideas come last. Then again, maybe the pressure is stimulating. When a frustrated pope asked Michelangelo whenever was he going to finish the damn Sistine ceiling, the artist replied: '*Quando potrò.*' ('When I can.') Whatever, this dilatoriness became a part of the reputation of the newly emancipated artist: time is needed for introspection.

You churn. And then you churn again. Possibly you do a little additional churning as well since you are confident that you will churn more and better tomorrow. A large part of the prodigal Picasso's work was cynical junk of the volitional kind, but the rest of it was genius of the smack-down, look-at-me, Dear-God-inspiring sort. The same can be said, with perhaps a little less enthusiasm, of Damien Hirst. You don't like what I have churned today? I'll churn again tomorrow.

But it's important to recognise a distinction between failures and mistakes. A failure is permanent; a mistake can and will be corrected. Failures are dispiriting; mistakes can, in the right hands, be stimulating. The sub-specification rubber O-rings which leaked and led to NASA's Space Shuttle calamity were failures. So too was Daimler's 1999 takeover of Chrysler: two manufacturers with such different engineering philosophies were unlikely to find productive synergies. But who knew?

The motor industry provides other examples of how beneficial tolerance of mistakes can be. Soichiro Honda said that success is simply that very small part of existence which was not humiliating calamity. You move from one mistake to the next with no less enthusiasm. Or, at least, that's what successful people do.

Put it this way: what would it be like *not* to learn from your mistakes? Success depends on error, thus there is a peculiar beauty in it. After discussing the matter with his unidentified oracular source, Miles Davis explained: 'If you're not making a mistake, it's a mistake.' In any case, he believed there are no wrong notes.

One thing is certain: we need to be wrong more often.

Conventional education tends to, or wants to, eradicate error. So does conventional business. And in eradicating error, in stigmatising mistakes, the spark of the fire stealers' motivation may be extinguished.

As Flaubert knew, success is a consequence, not a goal.

The joy of failure

We live in a society which is increasingly pre-occupied with success. At school, we have to get good exam results – and the school has to get good SATs reports. Then we have to get into a good university, where we must get a good degree, and then on to a high-earning job. (Presumably in a company which is doing better than its rivals.)

Then we will fall in love (preferably with someone who also has a great career), marry and have children. At which point, we will move house to be near a good school, where our kids will be pressured to get good exam results . . . and so on. Life is increasingly a treadmill of pressure to succeed.

'What's wrong with that?' I hear you cry. 'Isn't it normal to want success?'

Yes, it is normal to seek success, and without a willingness to strive, nothing would be accomplished. But the problem in today's society is that along with that lust for success is a paranoid fear of failure. If we don't get the grades we want or don't get to the university we want, we are already in life's dustbin. And we haven't had our twentieth birthday yet.

The real problem we have is not a desire to succeed: it's an equally strong desire not to fail. And fear of failure is an inhibiting, negative emotion which, paradoxically, is so constipating that it stops us succeeding.

Truly creative minds relish failure: they see it as a necessary stepping stone on the road to success. An imaginative chef, working on a signature dish for his new restaurant, doesn't expect to get it right first time. If he did, he'd suspect his own judgement. He will look forward to making endless variations of his idea, none of which are quite right, before he gets to what he really wants. Indeed this process of continued failure is part of the pleasure of creating, as well as the road to eventual success.

Similarly, all writers draft and redraft many times before they are satisfied with how they have expressed themselves. People who create see getting it wrong a few times as necessary staging posts on the way to getting it right.

Henry Ford understood this well when he said: 'Failure is simply the opportunity to begin again, this time more intelligently.'

Yet our society is not just obsessed with succeeding, but is also obsessed with not failing. To pursue success shows a normal and healthy degree of ambition. But to eschew failure is an altogether darker and more dangerous mindset, because it assumes success and failure can be uncoupled. The truth is that they are inexorably linked. To succeed you must first attempt; and an attempt may end in success but can also end in failure. So a reluctance to contemplate the possibility of failure removes the possibility of success.

J. K. Rowling sums this up eloquently: 'It is impossible to live without failing at something, unless you live so cautiously that you might as well not have lived at all – in which case, you fail by default.'

It's indicative of our hostility towards failure that if a politician changes heart over policy in the face of criticism, they are not praised for being a good listener but are attacked for a U-turn. This is seen as a kind of failure, not as an advance. But if the U-turn sends policy in a new direction which responds to constructive criticism, surely that is to be applauded?

The truth is that failure is an essential part of the creative process, and should be encouraged, not dismissed. The chef searching for that perfect recipe sees mistakes and disappointments not as failure but as experimentation. Similarly, the writer working on a novel sees drafting and redrafting not as a problem but as a journey towards their goal.

The reality is that we learn little from our successes, but we learn much from our mistakes. By defining what doesn't work, we narrow down our focus on what does work.

> ## The truth is that failure is an essential part of the creative process.

Writer's block & stage fright

▶ **John Lennon once advised me, after receiving an annoying adolescent letter where I solicited advice for relief of a constipated literary technique: 'I have the same problem in writing as you, but the answer is just LET IT ROLL.' Do it now, not later, is what the ur-Beatle meant.**

But creative personalities enjoy deferment and writer's block is a form of vanity. One of its sources is the complaisant notion that the moment is not propitious. But it is. 'I'll be able to do it better later' is a smug stratagem of avoidance. But maybe you won't. Writer's block ends when guilt overtakes lethargy and vanity. You learn to write by writing, not by pretending to be a tormented genius.

Jack Kerouac wrote his Beat Generation odyssey, *On the Road* (1957), using a vast roll of newsprint, spewing out as they drove. There were no 'pages'. It was an endless reel. As Marx knew, the means of production has its effects on consciousness. Maybe the lack of intimidating blank 'pages' was helpfully disinhibiting for Kerouac. Medium and message were all one as the trip spooled out and was recorded on continuous stationery.

Inhibition and procrastination play their part in writer's block, but Kerouac found a delivery system to defeat one and avoid the other. 'Spontaneous bop prosody', Andrew O'Hagan called it. But, as a matter of fact, this spontaneous bop prosody was thoughtfully conceived, carefully executed, scrupulously polished and meticulously edited.

The history of creativity has not a lot to say about spontaneity. Perhaps the fear of spontaneity builds writer's block in the first place.

Before the psychologist Edmund Bergler coined the term in 1947, F. Scott Fitzgerald had been the greatest martyr to writer's block, although Coleridge had complained about the 'indefinite indescribable terror' of not being able to write.

Fitzgerald had been famous at twenty-three, but he never got that second act in his American life. Instead, he was left with 'no choice, no road, no hope'. Bergler's specialism was self-defeating behaviour patterns and he was convinced that, while often hidden, masochism, the need to inflict pain or punishment on oneself, was a human universal. Hard, really, to imagine a point of view less conducive to creativity, although pain and pleasure are surely linked.

Writer's block is a Romantic idea, or, rather, has its origin in the Romantic view that creative inspiration blows like the breeze. Romantics did not believe in ten thousand hours of graft honing your craft, but, in Shelley's words, had to wait about for the 'inconstant wind' of inspiration. Another poet, Mallarmé, was so rarely visited by the wind, it took him nearly forty years to publish a mere sixty or so poems.

You learn to write by the act of writing itself. 'It is the beginning of the end', Dashiell Hammett said, 'when you discover that you have style.' Dickens knew this. He was a journalist before he was an artist. Anthony Trollope wrote 250 words every fifteen minutes. And because his proper job was working at the Post Office, he was only able to write between 5.00 and 8.30 a.m. In this way, he wrote forty-seven novels in thirty-five years. And so prolific was his facility that, during his morning stint, if he found he had finished one novel, he, without taking a breath, but dipping his pen in the inkpot and sighing deeply, would immediately start on another.

Trollope thought the writer a 'common labourer' and saw no need to tie wet towels around his sweating brow, nor sit at his desk for thirty-six hours without moving. In any case, his professional obligations would not allow it.

By contrast was Joseph Mitchell, the great prose-poet of mid-century New York, now enjoying retrospective cultish celebrity. In 1964 Mitchell published *Joe Gould's Secret*, itself about a blocked writer. For a whole thirty-six years he continued arriving, business-like, at his *New Yorker* desk and . . . writing not another word. Was this a fear of criticism, after *Joe Gould* had been so well received? We now call this second novel (or second album) syndrome: Harper Lee's *To Kill a Mockingbird* was published to huge acclaim in 1960 . . . and then *nada*.

But perhaps writer's block really is the medicalisation of vanity? When Bergler coined the term in 1947 the Great American Novel was becoming a media phenomenon. Everyone wanted to write one. And those who felt they were not quite up to it on current form found themselves blocked and, incidentally, craving pity and attention. To the prolific Anthony Burgess, a stern Mancunian Catholic, writer's block was exclusively a problem of pampered and spoiled Americans: only writers with Yaddo fellowships or Pulitzer grants or indulgent university sabbaticals could, surely, afford not to write.

Another classic in the anthology of literary blockage is Truman Capote and his long-deferred masterpiece *Answered Prayers* (1986). The title sardonically refers to St Teresa of Ávila's apothegm that, if there's one thing worse than unanswered prayers, it's the answered ones. With *Breakfast at Tiffany's* and *In Cold Blood*, Capote had justifiably secured a lofty reputation. The former a modern classic, the latter a pioneer blurring of reportage fact and literary fiction.

Capote signed a contract for *Answered Prayers* in 1966: it was to be an American Proust. He missed the first deadline in 1968 and subsequent ones offered by a harassed publisher in 1973, 1974 and 1977. He was eventually offered an additional $1 million to complete by 1980. Which he did not.

But he did describe his working practices, which were the very definition of displacement activity: rereading, rewriting and indexing his own letters, constant note-taking and writing the last chapter first 'because it's always good to know where you are going'. This chapter was memorably titled 'Father Flanagan's All-Night Nigger Queen Kosher Café': Capote was not afraid to offend. But he was afraid of something. Fragments were published in 1986, but it had been left unfinished at his death in 1984. His friend, Andy Warhol, said he never actually had any intention of completion.

Writing involves observation as well as imagination. And the connection that turns mere observation into art is the one that finds a word to match an experience. These words need not be complicated. In the following passage, 'ash' is the star. And here the terminally blocked Capote redeems himself. He might have had his problems with his unfinished masterpiece, but as a description of a taste, as an example of masterly writing, this passage cannot be bettered.

Even for those who dislike champagne, myself among them, there are two champagnes one can't refuse: Dom Pérignon and the even superior Cristal, which is bottled in a natural-colored glass that displays its pale blaze, a chilled fire of such prickly dryness that, swallowed, seems not to have been swallowed at all, but instead to have turned to vapors on the tongue and burned there to one damp sweet ash.

This is a perfect description. It is unprecedented; Capote copied no one. He relied only on his faithful response to an experience. Ash? That's what you get when you steal fire.

Meanwhile, Ritalin is prescribed for writer's block now that it has been identified as a form of ADHD. The psychoactive drug addresses glitches in brain chemistry and the limbic system, which have replaced missing muses or winds that do not blow as a source of this creative torment.

Invective & abuse: sh*t & c*nt

▶ **Johnnie Standing, the distinguished actor, has a fine expression of dismissal for a poor or incompetent literary performance. So-and-so, he says, 'couldn't write fuck on a shutter'. The absurdity and robustness combine to create a memorable insult. An internal alliteration helps too.**

On 10 December 1896 another actor walked on to the stage of Paris's Théâtre de l'Oeuvre and spoke the first word of Alfred Jarry's sensational play *Ubu Roi*. This was '*Merdre*!' The additional 'r' lifted the pronouncement above infantile smut, but the audience recognised sewage when they heard it. Jarry's 'sh*t', or maybe his 'shirt', anticipated Dada, surrealism and performance art. Sixty-five years later, Piero Manzoni created another sensation when he canned his own excrement.

Scatology and obscenity, invective and abuse are, when used with great art, stimulating. Henry Miller knew this. He created himself as a literary hero with the publication of *Tropic of Cancer* in Paris in 1934. Hitherto a marginal hanger-on in the French demi-monde, his first novel made his reputation. It contains a heroic and often-quoted exemplar of literary obscenity: 'There's a bone in my prick six inches long. I will ream out every wrinkle in your c*nt.' Quite so. With this breathtaking dirty talk, the world paid attention to Henry Miller.

The c-word retains an obstinate obscenity, hence even my use of an asterisk. In the Lady Chatterley trial, a clerk of the Department of

Public Prosecutions was required to analyse the text for the courts. It was found that 'fuck' or 'fucking' appeared thirty times, 'c*nt' fourteen, 'balls' thirteen, while 'shit' and 'arse' scored six each. This remarkable count brought remarkable attention to D. H. Lawrence's otherwise humdrum novel.

Over-familiarity can desensitise even the c-word. The lesson in creativity from Jarry, Miller and Lawrence is not about talking dirty, but about quotability. If you are going to say or write something, be certain it is f*cking memorable.

Besides scatology, invective and abuse can be useful means of making an impression. These are not quite the same as insults. Shakespeare's 'c*nt-bitten whoreson' and 'twat-scouring pimp' are magnificently rude, but also formulaic, since they were not agile responses to a circumstance.

Invective is more creative. It is a direct verbal attack, or, at least, that's how it was defined by Hugh Kingsmill in his classic *Anthology of Invective and Abuse* (1929). Thus, it is more considered and elaborate than a mere insult. Irony may evolve into invective, and in this journey loses its cool detachment because invective always has a jarring effect. Abuse may, Kingsmill says, be defined as 'colloquial invective'. Abuse is often called 'cheap', rather in the way that opinions are frequently dismissed as being 'mere', even if they are sincerely held and carefully considered vectors of thought.

Invective is a means to achieve an advantage by flamboyant rhetorical display. At its best, it is distinctively individual and often based in genuine emotion. And at its very best, driven by agile wit. There was a famous exchange in Parliament in 1763 when the Earl of Sandwich said to John Wilkes: 'Sir, you will either die on the gallows or of the pox.' Immediately, Wilkes replied: 'That, my lord, depends on whether I embrace your principles or your mistress.'

The poet Algernon Charles Swinburne resolved a literary dispute with R. W. Emerson in a memorable passage. 'I merely informed him, in language of the strictest reserve, that he was a hoary-headed and toothless baboon, who, first lifted into notice on the shoulder of Carlyle, now spits and splutters from a filthier platform of his own finding and fouling.' And he gently added: 'That is all I've said.'

James McNeill Whistler's *The Gentle Art of Making Enemies* (1890) is an anthology of his many high-concept squabbles, the one with John Ruskin being merely the best known. The critic accused the painter of 'flinging a pot of paint in the public's face'. In Whistler's art Ruskin saw 'the ill-educated conceit of the artist' approaching 'wilful imposture'.

Whistler replied: 'A life passed among pictures makes not a painter – else the policeman in the National Gallery might assert himself.' In the ensuing legal action, Whistler was awarded damages of a farthing.

Whistler and Wilde ran a dispute about plagiarism, the former thinking the latter something of a lifter. 'A poor thing, Oscar,' Whistler said, 'but, for once, I suppose your own.' Meanwhile, Wilde thought, 'With our James vulgarity begins at home, and should be allowed to stay there.'

Modern invective is often less elegant and may, on the whole, be said to be in decline, or retreating into 'mere' abuse. Objecting to a Camilla Long article about his client, Will Ferrell's publicist wrote, very publicly: 'Go fuck yourself, you slovenly piece of shit.' The journalist's response is not known. Of similar modest stature, at least when compared to Grattan's 1783 philippic against Flood, stands Kim Jong-un on Chang Song-thaek, who was accused of treason for not clapping with sufficient enthusiasm and for planting a statue of the North Korean dictator in too shady a place. Kim announced: 'Despicable scum, worse than a dog.'

This is not diplomatic language, but nor is it great invective.

When Caleb Crain gave Alain de Botton's *The Pleasures and Sorrows of Work* (2009) a review in which his enthusiasm was muted, it excited an extraordinarily abusive response from the author. Ignoring all that he had learnt from Proust in how to conduct your life with philosophical calm, ignoring even Oscar Wilde's comment on Whistler ('It is a trouble for any gentleman to have to notice the lucubrations of so ill-bred and ignorant a person'), de Botton accused his tormentor of 'vindictive lunacy' and wrote: 'You make it sound on your blog that your review is somehow a sane and fair assessment . . . [but] it is driven by an almost manic desire to bad-mouth.'

In an age of instantaneous global communication, the de Botton–Crain dispute was immediately public.

You have now killed my book in the United States . . . So that's two years of work down the drain in one miserable 900 word review . . . I will hate you till the day I die and wish you nothing but ill will in every career move you make.

This had little of the elegance, but all the publicity of the Ruskin–Whistler and Whistler–Wilde disputes.

Humbled by his ill-judged response to a review that was not even severely harsh, de Botton later admitted he was briefly 'deranged' and took down his subsequent tweets on the matter. Still, it was all noticed.

One of many uniquely useful Italian terms is '*furbizia*', untranslatable, but meaning approximately 'feral manners'. Feral language, whether calculated or spontaneous, often achieves a helpful notoriety. Scatology, obscenity, invective and abuse have their parts to play in achieving visibility for a person or a cause.

And no one intent on stealing fire wants to go unnoticed.

Mad, bad & fascinating to know:

inside the
creative mind

Uncle Jack's centrifuge

▶ **When I was a child, one of my great joys was our occasional visit to the workplace of my father's brother, Uncle Jack. My dad worked in a very conventional office – desks, chairs, filing cabinets, telephones. All the usual dull stuff. But Uncle Jack was a research biologist, and he worked in a laboratory with all kinds of weird and wonderful equipment that fascinated my seven-year-old mind.**

There were racks of test tubes, Bunsen burners, strangely shaped glass flasks – but the main attraction was the centrifuge. I'd never seen one before: a hollow metal cylinder, with test tubes hanging inside, which could (when Uncle Jack gave the word) whizz round at astonishing speed. I don't know any more about experimental biology today than I did then, but the concept Uncle Jack explained was simple: as the centrifuge accelerated, so the suspended test tubes flew outwards from the vertical to the horizontal, and under this pressure the contents of the test tubes separated, so making them much more susceptible to analysis.

What caused this to happen, it was explained to me, was centrifugal force, a phenomenon in which physical bodies tend to fly out from the centre towards the edge. It was also explained to me that there was a counter-balancing phenomenon, centripetal force, in which bodies tend to rush in towards the centre. As a child, I was not the least bit interested in the physics of all this, but I was utterly excited by the sight and sound of the centrifuge at full pelt.

As an adult, the memory stayed with me, and I came to realise that it provides an astonishingly good metaphor for how we are as people. Most people have centripetal personalities: that is to say, they instinctively tend to gravitate to the centre ground, to the consensus view. In the main, people want to move, attitudinally, to where most other people are. This can be described, a little sneeringly perhaps, as 'the herd instinct'. Indeed, two great nineteenth-century philosophers, Kierkegaard and Nietzsche, both wrote critically about the human tendency to group together, and to reinforce each other.

However, it's hard to imagine what kind of world it would be if people did not tend to move towards a shared view. Without some kind of wish for consensus, some search for the centre ground, we could only exist in a state of anarchy and chaos. Most of us are, for better or for worse, centripetal personalities, and the world would be an unmanageable place if that were not so. A willingness to agree on what's to be done is at the heart of any ordered society. So let's be grateful for the centripetal instinct.

But some personalities are centrifugal: far from seeking to share the common view, for these types it seems to be a point of honour to shun it. These are people who are constantly rejecting the accepted orthodoxies, always searching for a different way of doing things. This does not make for an easy life, but the centrifugal personality has little expectation of that anyway. Their avoidance of the conventional wisdom is bound to isolate them, to make them something of an outcast. As Nietzsche said: 'The individual has always had to struggle to keep from being overwhelmed by the tribe.'

Of course, there are thousands of other dimensions in personality types – shy versus outgoing, confident versus self-doubting, arrogant versus humble, thoughtful versus impulsive, and so on. But the distinction between centripetal personalities (that's most of us) and the centrifugal minority is key to understanding creativity.

Why?

Because the core of creativity is about finding new ideas, finding different solutions. Which of course means ideas and solutions that are not current now, not generally accepted today. Inevitably, the creative thinker is endlessly rejecting current methods and pushing for some original, as yet unimagined, concept. We mostly drift towards the centre, but the artist pushes out to the far limits.

The language we use reflects this phenomenon. We describe avant-garde work as 'edgy' as if we see it on the very edge, the outer perimeter of life's centrifuge. Whereas a politician who seeks a broad consensus will be described as 'centrist', and already we have an image of someone who is pragmatic and willing to compromise, but unlikely to be imaginative or risk-taking. The clichés 'pushing the envelope' and 'thinking outside the box' both suggest the need to fly out, like the test tubes in the centrifuge, beyond the boundaries of our contained world.

Don't assume that a centrifugal personality is an antisocial one. The centrifugal mind rejects existing ideas, but that's not the same as rejecting people. Picasso had a truly centrifugal mind: when he and Braque created the concept of cubism they took art to a place it had never been to before. But in his personal life, Picasso was a highly social animal, with a wide range of friends, and nearly as wide a range of mistresses. To prove the point, he didn't die in solitude, but at one of his own dinner parties.

Creativity has to be centrifugal, to discard today's precepts, in the search for the truly original. This is why many find contemporary art so problematic: it must by definition fly in the face of what we're used to, what we feel comfortable with.

Don't think that only applies to Tracey Emin's unmade bed. When

Goya was painter to the Spanish royal court in the early nineteenth century, he got into all sorts of trouble with the Spanish Inquisition because he painted otherwise identical pictures of the same woman: but in one (*Maja vestida*) she is clothed, in the other (*Maja desnuda*) she is naked. The effect is profoundly erotic, and so was spectacularly controversial at the time. It wasn't the conventional way to paint. There was public outrage, and the Spanish Inquisition bounced Goya out of his role as painter to the royal court. An earlier Spanish painter to the royal court, Velásquez, painted *The Rokeby Venus*, an image of a naked woman with her back to us. Convention at the time dictated that nudity in art was utterly *de trop*. Velásquez, like Goya, found himself mightily unpopular with the inquisition. Today, of course, the Velásquez hangs proudly in London's National Gallery and the two Goyas are equally admired in the Prado in Madrid. The point is that art must explore the unfamiliar, and so is bound, good or bad, to be the victim of controversy when it first appears.

That does not, of course, mean that all controversial art is good: far from it. But it does mean that new ideas will inevitably be centrifugally generated, will challenge existing conventions, and so will be controversial: at least until they are no longer new.

If we accept that there is a centrifugal force at work in creativity, what are the implications?

First, you shouldn't expect highly creative people to be easy bedfellows. It's in their nature to shun conventional wisdom and even to disdain conventional values. Their originality is rooted in a rejection of what they see around them. To quote Nietzsche again, 'Creativity is an endless struggle against the status quo.'

This mindset often expresses itself in behaviour which is at best

> **'Creativity is an endless struggle against the status quo.'**

eccentric, at worst downright antagonistic. Bob Dylan's grudging reaction to being awarded the 2016 Nobel Prize for Literature, eventually sending someone else to the ceremony to make his speech for him, hovered somewhere between insensitively ungracious and downright rude. As for eccentricity, Salvador Dalí would be a fine example, with his absurdly mannered waxed moustache, his ivory-handled cane and his preposterous utterances.

It doesn't have to be like that: Dalí's contemporary, René Magritte, presented himself in the most conservative way. You could easily have mistaken him for a provincial bank manager. And there have been plenty of creative giants who were charm personified. But nonetheless, creative people are, generally, more likely to be prickly, difficult to handle, dissatisfied with everything. But there is a logic to that: if you weren't dissatisfied, you wouldn't seek to create something better.

Second, if creativity is a force which flies away from the centre, rejecting existing values and existing ideas of quality, it makes one ask, 'How do we judge what is good?'

If you're expecting a quick, clear answer to this one, you're going to be disappointed. It's a problem which has confounded philosophers, let alone you and me, for generations. There is an intriguing book, *The Art Question*, in which the British philosopher Nigel Warburton attempts to define quality in art. His ultimate conclusion to the central question of 'What is art?' is simply to say that it '. . . is probably not answerable'.

I'd only suggest that if you want to be sure what's good and what isn't, just wait a hundred years. As creative ideas are produced by the centrifugal mind, it's inevitable that they will flout the standards and values of their time. So you must let time pass, and judge them with the perspective of history. It's only when you take a long view that you can really see what has worth.

We shouldn't forget that immediately before the 2008 banking crisis, the consensus among experts in the financial world was that things looked good and the Western world was prospering. How wrong they were. But that was the conventional wisdom at the time.

As Kierkegaard said: 'Truth always rests with the minority.' Usually we need a good dose of historical hindsight before we can make a value judgement that we can trust.

> 'Truth always rests with the minority.'

If you want to see the tension between centripetal and centrifugal mindsets played out, read Ionesco's absurdist drama *Rhinoceros*. A resident of a small French town claims that he has seen a rhinoceros in the town: a very centrifugal opinion. He is vilified by others in the village – until they start seeing rhinos too. Eventually, those that have seen a rhinoceros become the majority view, and the few who haven't are stigmatised. It's a metaphor for how we can all be victims of the herd instinct, the centripetal norm.

The power of this herd instinct can also be demonstrated by the way we look at left-handed people. The best estimates suggest that about 10 per cent of the world's population is left-handed, so we left-handers (yes, I am one, guilty as charged) are a small minority. But it obviously doesn't matter a fig whether one is right-handed or left-handed. Or does it? Think about the language we use. Someone who is socially awkward is described as 'gauche' – the French word for 'left'. Anyone or anything which is a bit creepy is described as 'sinister' – the Latin word for 'left'. When giving directions, if we want to say 'continue straight ahead' we'll say 'keep right on'. Similarly, the French for 'straight ahead' is *'tout droit'*, or 'all right' in English. Vocabulary relating to 'right' (the majority behaviour) is loaded with positive meaning, while vocabulary relating to 'left' (the minority behaviour) is loaded with negative meaning. Before you dismiss these linguistic pointers as relics from a prejudiced past, consider that very new invention: Tinder. There, to discard someone who fails to tempt you, you swipe to the left, but to reel in someone who looks hot, you swipe to the right. Right-handedness, which clearly has no intrinsic merit alongside left-handedness, is nonetheless seen to be the correct way: simply because it's what most people do. It's an example of the way society regards the behaviour of the majority as somehow superior, regardless of the circumstances. Herd instinct is a force not to be under-rated. And this force is essentially centripetal.

Which is why the centrifugal, creative mind is endlessly at odds with the mainstream.

The creative person, like the first man to sight the rhinoceros, is forever destined to be an outsider, flung to the outer edge of society's centrifuge.

How can this insight help us in the fight to generate creative ideas?

A good start is to avoid research like chickens avoid foxes. The whole point of consumer research is to define what people think and do now. In other words, it is the definitively centripetal activity: it shows us where the current centre of opinion is. It gives us a wonderful view of where we are now – and therefore absolutely no insight into where the next new direction might take us.

Henry Ford, the genius who democratised the motor car and so changed all our lives, had a healthy contempt for market research. When asked why he never did any research, he tartly replied, 'If I asked people what they wanted, they'd say faster horses.'

It's not just a good joke, it's a brilliantly shrewd observation too. Ford understood that in research people

'If I asked people what they wanted, they'd say faster horses.'

tended to view a better future as an improved version of what they have now. But sometimes the future hinges on a totally innovative concept, which owes nothing to what has gone before. The affordable motor car – Ford's gift to the world – was just that. A centrifugal thought if ever there was one.

The kind of people who like doing market research to guide new ideas are themselves highly centripetal in personality, so they inevitably relish analysing the current consensus. And they fail to see that creativity depends on a huge, centrifugal leap from that consensus to a new and unimagined place.

If we are to produce creative ideas, or if we are to respond well to other people's creative ideas, we must abandon the centripetal values of the many and learn to fall in love with the centrifugal values of the few.

Eureka! Caricatures of genius

▶ **How to describe the steam and electricity of thought? It is to the Roman architectural theorist Vitruvius that we owe the story of Archimedes receiving his famous insight into displacement theory and yelling 'Eureka!' while in the bath (apparently alone).**

Eureka means 'I have found it!' but, so excited was Archimedes by this creative revelation, he immediately lost it and went running naked through the streets of Syracuse. Vitruvius was writing two centuries after this peculiar incident, but it might even be true. Whatever, it has given us an enduring image of how genius operates. It's what used to be called *furor poeticus*, a fever dream, a creative ecstasy, divine madness; creativity was sourced in the gods. And, quite often, it drives its possessors mad.

A creative genius does not submit to ordinary laws: he writes his own. Discussing his development of information theory and the binary system, which made modern computing possible, Claude Shannon explained that he simply had to *invent* the maths needed to prove his point. The maths required simply did not exist before.

Einstein was not in the bath when he received his famous inspiration about relativity, nor was he riding a beam of light, but in a slow-moving tram in Bern gazing at the Zytglogge, the thirteenth-century clock tower. Time travel has several interpretations. But flashes of insight are actually rather rare. For every very brilliant flash he occasionally experienced, Einstein had some very long dull moments in the Patent Office. Discovery occurs slowly at first, but then accelerates. But it's hardly ever explicable. 'I just ignored an axiom,' he said. People who steal fire often enjoy a perversity in accounting for it.

After Archimedes, Einstein is the great caricature of genius . . . a role to which he contributed more than his scientific insights. Wacky haircuts, antic expressions and an unruly romantic life all contributed to our expectations. The achievement was prodigal: in 1905 alone, when he was a 26-year-old clerk, he wrote four papers which rivalled Newton in explaining the mechanics of the universe. The *New York Times* treated him like a Second Coming or, at least, as a Jewish saint. One headline said: 'Lights All Askew in the Heavens. Einstein Theory Triumphs'. No doubt, Einstein's attractive personality and his distinctive visual identity contributed to his easy popular acceptance as a creative genius, even if popular understanding of his Great Idea remains modest.

Naturally, people were curious about Einstein's brain. Not unaware of publicity and the personal advantages it can bring, he agreed to EEG investigations at Massachusetts General Hospital in 1951. Continuing the physical analysis of his mysterious mind, on his death in 1955, Thomas Harvey made prosciutto-thin slices of Einstein's brain at Princeton Hospital. These are now preserved in the National Museum of Health and Medicine at Silver Spring, Maryland, have been most helpfully digitised and are available as an app. Meanwhile, an ophthalmologist called Henry Abrams claimed the great man's eyeballs.

Unscrupulous regimes often believe that pathology might explain creative genius, that an investigation of organs might reveal the mysterious seat of creativity: a busy little weevil at the core of our being. Biological explanations inevitably err into scientifically flawed and disagreeable racial theories. Hitler, for example, declared in *Mein Kampf* (1925) that 'true genius is always inborn and never cultivated'.

Ever practical, the Soviet Union believed investigative surgery could discover what makes us creative. Moscow's Institut Mozga (the Moscow Brain Institute) examined Lenin's brain to find 'the material substrate of genius', a process that required it to be cut into thirty thousand slices. It was found that the pyramidal cells in the third layer of the central cortex were superhumanly developed. Hence, the revolution of 1917 and a subsequent culture devoted to tractors.

Stalin's brain was examined here too, although the examiner, one Vladimir Bekhterev, disappeared when his investigations came to the scientific conclusion that Lenin's brutal successor was paranoid. Be that as it may, Mozga was busy collecting, slicing and analysing creative brains until 1989: Gorky's, Mayakovsky's and Eisenstein's are included in its disturbing archives. Glasnost brought an end to this study.

But what makes great men great is not understood, no matter how you slice it. Genius is not hereditary. Nor is creativity. It's actually not in the DNA. Nor, so far as we can yet determine, in slices of the brain or in preserved eyeballs. Einstein had a schizophrenic son of no explicit talent and, for another example, Hemingway's children were all disturbed and none was a writer (although one was a colourful and imaginative transvestite, revealing a taste for self re-invention). So where exactly is it?

'Before creativity,' Freud said, 'the psychoanalyst must lay down his arms.' It is good to have psychoanalysts lay down their clunky arms because there are cultural explanations of creativity. Although it was known to the ancients, the idea of genius evolved in the eighteenth century to explain the extraordinary achievements (and often extraordinary behaviour) of creative individuals.

Genius became a secular religion in the Enlightenment: the intellectual equivalent of the discovery of steam power and electricity. Genius is contemporary with the notions of personality and privacy. And other new concepts of self. It was what Jefferson called 'natural aristocracy'.

Genius is not the same as wisdom. Francis Galton described a genius as 'a man to whom the world deliberately acknowledges itself largely indebted'.

Wisdom has no need to be creative. Wisdom is about emotional control, self-knowledge and pragmatism. Light-bulb moments in the bath or elsewhere are less easy to explain. But it is also true that creative people have little use for emotional control, self-knowledge or pragmatism.

There is a wonderful oddness about stories of geniuses' Eureka moments: Giotto as a peasant boy found drawing a perfect circle in the Tuscan dust; Leonardo staring at stains of water intrusion and puddles, procrastinating all the while. Because, as Vasari noted, 'men of lofty genius sometimes accomplish the most when they work least.' Or Georg Perec's peculiar novel without the character 'e'. Padgett Powell's novel comprising only questions. Then there are clever conceptual flips: Thoreau saying candles illuminate the darkness while electricity destroys it. Donald Judd saying Philip Johnson was 'discreetly vulgar'.

But sometimes the genius works hard. Rubens and Bernini, for example. Judd again on Bernini: '[He] made religion, supposedly the nature of the world, personal. And so religious art and architecture ended; after that it was sentimental and academic.' Judd, while evoking a divine connection, means that genius transforms and even destroys traditions. There is a necessary impulse towards chaos . . . even if it is a version of chaos that Biblical Creation put beyond our reach.

If you accept that, then 'sanity' is not always helpful here. And if you look at classic modern art, cubism, for example, it is easy to make a connection between the multiple viewpoints, the fragmentation and the defiance of authority and the symptoms of classic schizophrenia.

There is an enlarging body of literature which makes a credible scientific case for the link between genius and madness, a connection that in any case goes back as far as Seneca. No matter, mental illness is not a reliable test for the presence of genius. As Charles Lamb said: 'It is impossible . . . to conceive of a mad Shakespeare.' When Havelock Ellis, the pioneer sexologist, in his *Study of British Genius* (1904), trawled *The Dictionary of National Biography* for geniuses, he was disappointed to find that only 4.2 per cent of them appeared to be insane. Most, at least by the *Dictionary*'s account, were sensible and rational.

Still, many of the informal definitions of the creative personality also sound like psychiatric diagnoses. It is, for example, presently thought that sufferers from psychosis are able to entertain conflicting thoughts simultaneously. And that's a very creative thing to do – rather as Einstein thought you could be stationary and moving at the speed of light at the same time. In one recent test, people diagnosed with bipolar disorder were able to generate four times as many word associations as the norm. That's creative too.

The etymology of 'genius' is from the Latin *gignere*, which means 'to generate'. Genius is also the art of editing, of knowing what to overlook or ignore. And if you are a genius, you must accommodate two apparently conflicting ideas simultaneously. As they say in Zen, 'Whatever is true, the opposite is truer.'

'Whatever is true, the opposite is truer.'

The Book of Revelation: how Michelangelo set figures free

Michelangelo was so prodigally talented, so inventive, so incomparably skilled in the practice of all the visual arts, so restlessly energetic, so argumentative, he appeared superhuman to his contemporaries.

He even – taking a break from architecture, frescoes and sculpture of unequalled beauty and force – wrote perfectly passable poems. Mortal or practical constraints were as irrelevant to him as social conventions of politeness or manners. He operated so far beyond human limits that people assumed he was possessed by God. They even called him *Il Divino*. The divine consultant.

He had special properties. While most of us would look, unmoved, at the surface of an enormous and forbidding block of stone, Michelangelo's vision penetrated it. He saw what others did not see. Within, he believed, every heavy, dead block of marble there is a living statue waiting to escape. It was his creative task to set this person, for it was a living thing, free.

Sculptors necessarily engage with the hard facts of working in stone. Michelangelo preferred to source his from Monte Altissimo in the Apuan Alps, a marble of compact grain, homogenous and crystalline.

But there was something else in the yards of Florence's Opera del Duomo, the cathedral workshop. This was a forbidding block, eighteen feet tall. Simone da Fiesole had started work on it years before, but got no further than drilling a useless hole, which compromised the future utility of the block. And then he gave up. In 1464 Agostino di Duccio resumed art's assault on this marble, but was deterred by the imperfections and stopped work. Then in 1476 Antonio Rossellino took up the hammer and chisel, only to drop them again promptly.

The unloved block, scarred with half-hearted false starts by mediocre artists, now sat neglected for twenty-five years . . . until Michelangelo came across it. He did not see unfortunate drill holes, tentative chisel marks: 'I saw the angel in the marble and carved until I set him free.' This angel was the David, the uncircumcised King of the Jews, eerily proportioned, frankly rather freakish, but an eternal exemplar of male beauty, now in the Accademia.

In *The Lives of the Artists* (1550, first English edition 1908), Giorgio Vasari, the gossip columnist of the Renaissance and one of the greatest boosters in all history, calls Michelangelo *divino* more than twenty times. You also find words like *stupendo! stupore! meraviglia! mirabilia!* There were many ways to Michelangelo's genius. 'The Great Ruler of Heaven decided to send to earth a genius universal in each art': thus, Vasari. Michelangelo was also possessed of 'true moral philosophy' and a 'sweet, poetic spirit'. He was, however, also unkempt, insanitary and had irregular habits.

Certainly, Vasari's account of Michelangelo has shaped our perceptions and expectations of the creative type: an eccentric outsider, a man apart, driven by unearthly passions and with practical skills of execution to match. But most especially of having a vision.

Being able to see a pattern or a possibility invisible to others may be a defining aspect of creativity. It is sometimes said that talent can hit a

target, but genius can see a target no one else can. 'The greatest danger', Michelangelo believed, 'is not that our aim is too high and we miss it, but that it is too low and we reach it.'

In pop culture, Michelangelo has an equivalent status to Einstein: an irregular, compulsive, incomparable genius-creative. The two also shared a capacity to see what others could not, even if it was hidden in plain sight. When his father gave him a compass as a present, Einstein became hypnotically engrossed with the instrument. The flickering mag-

netised needle was not a guide to the cardinal points, but a key that unlocked the deepest mysteries of the universe.

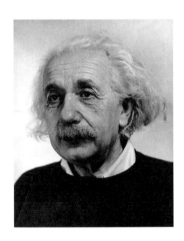

In another interpretation of creativity, Michelangelo and Einstein might have been said to be inspired by Muses who live in the heavens. But Muses are, probably, more earthbound. Muses, instead, lurk in parts of the mind inaccessible to ordinary folk, but to which Michelangelo and Einstein had easy and rapid access.

The critic Norman Podhoretz's accomplishments are fewer, perhaps, than those of Michelangelo and Einstein, but his confessional autobiography *Making It* (1967) is a masterly account of his own self-invention . . . perhaps the most interesting creative task of them all. Podhoretz made stealing fire his life's work.

Interestingly, Podhoretz describes the writer's inspiration as something similar to the sculptor's stone or the physicist's compass:

'The writer does not experience his writing as an act of creation; he experiences it as an act of discovery: it *comes* or *happens* or is *given* to him, and when it does, he recognizes it at once for his own.'

Creativity is a state of mind. And that state must be fluid in every sense. It involves openness and acceptance. It does not involve barriers, definitions or compartments; revelations can best be perceived and accommodated by minds that are not empty, but open. And these minds are able to reveal things others cannot even imagine.

How many brains do you have?

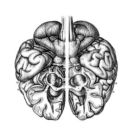

If you look at yourself, it's very obvious that you've got two feet, two ears, two eyes, two nostrils . . . I could go on. And in each case, the one on the left works just like the one on the right. But if you could look inside your head (a rather ghastly thought, I agree) you'd see that you also have two brains: a left brain and a right brain. We talk about 'the brain' as if it is one unit, but it's not. It's actually two distinct, separate hemispheres. But what is startling about the left brain and the right brain is that the two halves operate quite differently and have different functions. The left eye sees the same as the right eye; the left foot walks the same as the right foot. But it's not like that with your two brains – they do different things, and they do them in different ways.

What has this neuroscience got to do with creativity? More than you might expect, is the answer. Doctors have observed for a long time that if one side of the brain switches off – because of a stroke in that hemisphere, for example – some activities grind to a sudden halt, yet others carry on as if nothing has happened. So they could identify which functions are controlled by the right brain and which by the left. From this, we've learnt that in terms of body activity, paradoxically it is the left brain that manages the right side and the right brain that manages the left.

Recent advances in diagnostic technology, such as EEG recording and MRI scanning, have taken this branch of medicine to a new level: it's now possible to study activity in the brain and link it to behaviour.

We should beware of over-simplifying. It's an immensely complex topic. In Iain McGilchrist's brilliant study of the subject, *The Master and His Emissary*, he says: 'It has been estimated that there are more connections within the human brain than there are particles in the known universe.' Think about that for a moment.

The two brains don't just manage different halves of the body's motor functions, they're wired differently and they handle different aspects of thinking. The left brain is wired more like a serial processor, concentrates on logical and analytical thinking, and is strong on detail. The right brain is wired more like a parallel processor, doesn't care for detail, and concentrates on more imaginative thinking. The left brain is precise, and identifies issues in isolation, while the right brain is empathetic and understands context. Visual ideas are inspired in the right brain.

Most important, from the point of view of understanding creativity, the right brain has a talent – which the left brain lacks – for making unlikely connections. It can make an imaginative leap from where we are now, and take us to a different place. The left brain thinks vertically, the right brain thinks laterally.

The two halves of the brain are both working for us all the time, and they are connected by a bundle of nerve tissue called the corpus callosum. (Digressing for a moment, it is interesting to note that this body is larger in female brains than in male, and it has been speculated that this more potent link between the two brains in women may explain why women are better at multi-tasking.) The corpus callosum serves to connect the two halves but, intriguingly, it also serves to inhibit the transfer of information as well as to promote it. It's a bit like a marriage guidance counsellor who knows when to keep the two partners apart, as well as when to push them together. This only gives more emphasis to the very different character of right and left brains.

If you wanted to summarise this character difference in childishly simplistic terms, you could say that the left brain is better at sums, but the right brain is better at poetry. Simplistic that may be, but it's not that far from the truth. The left brain's fundamental talent is its ability to analyse what is there; the right brain's fundamental talent is to imagine what could be there.

We can clearly see a distinction between logical, rational thought and imaginative, creative thought. They are very different types of thinking, and they emanate from opposed hemispheres of the brain. Equally, some personality types are left-brain biased – logical, but not that imaginative – while other personalities are right-brain biased – good at ideas, less good at detail and organisation. This starts to explain why people in business often struggle with the creative world. The chief executive of a major corporation will be good at studying spreadsheets of costs and identifying numerical strengths and weaknesses in the business. But show that same person an idea for an advertising campaign and they'll be in a foreign country where they don't speak the language.

This explains why large companies like to use market research to test advertising ideas: they want to subject an idea, which is essentially qualitative and subjective, to an assessment which is essentially quantitative and objective. It's a bit like judging the worth of a painting by weighing it.

It's a daft idea, but people still do it – because left-brain minds feel threatened by right-brain ideas, and so need to measure them in left-brain terms. That is why TV commercials (and I know there are some notable exceptions) are nowadays generally so banal. With creative ideas being subjected to more and more market research, the values of right-brain imagination have been censored by left-brain logic.

We can explore this issue biologically. When the brain perceives new information, it releases noradrenaline, a chemical which works as a neurotransmitter and prepares us for action. But this happens mostly in the right brain. So, at a level of basic brain chemistry, it is clear that the right brain is primed to be more receptive to new ideas than the left brain. Knowing this, it's little surprise that people whose personalities seem to be left-brain dominated are grudging about embracing new thinking.

> **At a level of basic brain chemistry, it is clear that the right brain is primed to be more receptive to new ideas than the left brain.**

How does all this neuroscience affect the way we live, the way we judge ideas, the way we generate ideas?

First, we mustn't expect those who are logical and linear in their thinking to be good at creating new ideas or good at responding to new ideas. It's just not in their nature. After all, you wouldn't ask a fish to run.

Second, left-brain thought tends to be self-referring: in other words, it judges by its own standards and it's not adept at taking a different perspective. So left-brain types in a group tend to reinforce each other. That's why the business 'brainstorm' is inevitably a failure. We've explored the underlying absurdity of the brainstorm in more depth in another chapter; for now, suffice it to say that when you recruit a group of people with similar mindsets and ask them to think differently, it's not going to happen. Each will confirm the prejudices of the other, while no one will search for a different path.

The key to resolving this problem is to expose left-brain types to right-brain types, and vice versa, as much as you dare. You aren't going to get people suddenly to switch personality, but you will see them start to learn from someone of an alternative mindset.

In the UK's 2016 referendum on whether to leave the EU, it was revealing that the greatest level of hostility to migrants came from those parts of the country with the lowest levels of immigration. In contrast, London, which has an astonishingly diverse population, voted overwhelmingly to stay in the EU with its open borders.

So, familiarity doesn't have to breed contempt: it can often breed understanding.

An example of this is the habit in advertising agencies for copywriters and art directors to work as a two-person team. Both of them have to be imaginative, but the copywriter uses words, which must inevitably be structured into some pattern, while the art director uses imagery, and an image can stand on its own, and convey its own story. Hence the saying 'a picture is worth a thousand words'. Consequently, the art director would usually be more strongly right brain than the writer. (Though, before some aggrieved writer complains, both have to be imaginative.) So, each of the pair would have a somewhat different mindset from the other: and when the personal chemistry is good, this pairing of slightly unalike minds can produce very creative results.

Don't imagine that in this pairing the writer always does the words, and the art director always does the pictures. On the contrary, the point is that the two of them produce one concept: but it's a better concept because of the cross-fertilisation between them.

Thus, putting people of differing attitudes together can be creatively fertile. But the reverse is also true: people of similar attitudes don't work well together creatively. If you want to see an example – on a horrific scale – of what can go wrong when you team up people who all have similar mindsets, remind yourself of the 2008 banking crisis. Groups of very clever people brought the Western world close to bankruptcy. Why? Because they were all good, left-brain thinkers. So they could see the numbers – but they couldn't see beyond the numbers to the wider picture.

What if the assumptions on which the numbers were based were false? Assumptions, for instance, like 'people on low incomes will repay their debt'. This was a question no one asked, until it was too late. If the banks had a few right-brain thinkers on board, people who could think more laterally, then the crucial question might have been asked in time to do something about it. The banking crisis wasn't a failure of logic: those left-brain bankers could analyse and understand exactly what was happening at the time. It was a failure of imagination. Those same bankers lacked the right-brain ability to stand back and imagine what might happen tomorrow.

This demonstrates that the difference between left- and right-brain activity is much more than some arcane aspect of neuroscientific study – it's something which affects how we all live and act.

Being contrarian & defeating habits

George Moore, the Irish poet and novelist, who studied art in Paris in the 1870s, once wrote: 'I remember Manet's reply when I questioned him about the pure violet shadows which . . . he was beginning to introduce into his pictures. "One year one paints violet and people scream, and the following year every one paints a great deal more violet." ' No interest in adapting to expectations here. The poet Schiller kept rotten apples in his desk whose pungent aroma, he said, encouraged his art. Where others smelt decay, Schiller found his muse.

Thus the contrarian nature of the creative personality. It is sometimes said, by those who seek metaphors in plumbing, that people can be either radiators or drains. Artists are usually radiators, although, like drains, they do absorb everything put into them. Test yourself: do you see holes or bridges? Opportunities or problems? Do you want to see what's around the corner? Are you a unifier or a revolutionary?

It's often said that there is no surer sign of stupidity than repeating patterns of behaviour and expecting different results. If you find banging your head against a bush-hammered concrete wall is painful, then stop. Intelligence is, by contrast, behaviour that is adaptively variable. Creative intelligence especially so.

The architect Louis Kahn used to enjoy talking to his building materials. This may sound mad, but the results are there to be admired. You speak to the brick and the brick replies, Kahn said. In this way were some of the twentieth century's greatest buildings realised. In Ahmedabad, for example, Kahn's bricks told him to build the most sensational plastic essay in light and air.

Creative people see things differently. And they also hear differently, although Arnold Schoenberg's remark applies to all art forms. In fact, to all behaviours. Schoenberg once said: 'When a piece of music is too long, you can't shorten it.' Ends become beginnings, walls become doors, windows become mirrors, logic becomes nonsense and those same ends don't have to justify the means, or vice versa.

Frank Lloyd Wright, another great architect, was also a great contrarian. To justify his inventions, he rewrote history: the Renaissance, in his view, was a setting sun which was mistaken for a dawn. Patience and humility were not Wright's distinguishing characteristics, nor often those of any artist.

Creative contrarians do not seek approval or consensus. Even Frank Sinatra could not have made a hit out of a song called 'I Did It Your Way'. Creative types block metaphors, ignore axioms, abhor customs and disdain the ordinary. Except, that is, when the ordinary is something exceptional.

The flip method is a part of this fight against the seductive power of routine. You look at the status quo and think how much more interesting it would be to have it inverted. Thus, a cartoon in the *New Yorker* shows a hopeful young man propositioning, in the days when such things were possible, an attentive and eager young woman. He says: 'OK, so we'll have sex and if that works out we'll go out for a nice dinner and maybe a movie.' Thus, the world turned upside-down.

A splendid example of the flip method is Joni Mitchell's beautiful 1967 song 'Both Sides Now'. Mitchell was a folk-rock artiste of uncertain potential who found herself on board a plane with a copy of Saul Bellow's 1959 novel *Henderson the Rain King*, recommended by a friend. Here, the anti-hero Henderson finds himself flying over Africa, looking at the cloudscape. And Bellow muses: when people could look up and down at clouds they should not be afraid to die. We are, he seems to be saying, a little like ye gods.

Mitchell found herself looking at the cloudscape too. And perhaps she thought: less than a century before, no one had ever seen clouds from above. But now a 737 or a DC-9 gave any travellers a superlative vision denied to emperors and princes, known only to gods in the past. In this way was a brilliant conceit formed. Mitchell had seen both sides of the clouds.

One aspect of clouds was imagistic, fantastical and whimsical:

Rows and flows of angel hair
And ice-cream castles in the air
And feather canyons everywhere . . .

But there was a darker side to clouds as well. Clouds can be dispiriting as well as inspiring. Creative people always, but always, see alternatives:

But now they only block the sun
They rain and snow on everyone
So many things I could have done
But clouds got in my way.

And then in the concluding verses, Mitchell does another ingenious flip. She exchanges 'clouds' for 'love', so it goes: 'I've looked at love from both sides now.' And in the mordant conclusion applying to atmospheric vapour as well as to romance, she sings:

**It's clouds' illusions I recall
I really don't know clouds at all.**

Just replace 'clouds' with 'love' and you have a perfect song, created by an accidental insight and a brilliant creative flip.

'Move fast and break things' are Mark Zuckerberg's watchwords. Facebook was not built by a timid man. Reviewing his career, the painter Lucian Freud told the critic Martin Gayford: 'It was marvellous being taken seriously for behaving ridiculously.' The chef Grant Achatz of Alinea in Chicago asks bogglingly ridiculous questions of the food he prepares. 'Can we make cheese that floats?' Asking mad questions takes you interesting places, which a docile acceptance of circumstances will not. You will not find better evidence of how the creative 'character' sees the world than Zuckerberg, Freud or Achatz. Unless you want to include 'I learn by going where I have to go' by Theodore Roethke.

Jazz is a disruptive music form and supplies many useful metaphors of creativity, as explained by Frank J. Barrett in *Yes to the Mess* (2012), a book published by those great advocates of untidiness, *Harvard Business Review*. Jazz positively seeks out instability, novelty and disorder. Barrett, who once toured with the Tommy Dorsey Orchestra, says there are lots of 'surprising leadership lessons from jazz'. Miles Davis, for example, used to listen to what everybody else was playing and then play what was missing.

Certainly, routines and habits form roadblocks on the route to discovery, yet creative people, while anarchic in many ways, often acquire strict and unbending habits. Jonathan Swift, Samuel Johnson, Ludwig van Beethoven, Charles Dickens, Henrik Ibsen, Giacomo Rossini, Igor Stravinsky is a list of workplace obsessives to which we can confidently add the name of Steven P. Jobs. Musing on this, psychiatrist Anthony Storr asked: 'At what point does a concern with precision become pathological?' Perhaps when Steve Jobs decided he did not want screw-heads to be visible.

Balzac, fuelled by unusual amounts of coffee, the *carburant des grands artistes*, went to bed at 6 p.m. in order to wake at 1 a.m. and write for a further seven hours. He would then sleep until 9.30 a.m., rise and write continuously until 4 p.m. Then, for the next two hours, he would receive guests, take a bath, a promenade, have dinner and then go to bed. Only to repeat the following day. And on.

Graham Greene wrote five hundred words a day. It's safe to say that Balzac and Greene thought inspiration was for amateurs. Writing is a professional task, like bricklaying. And, like bricklaying, there are quotas. 'The professional', Dizzy Gillespie once said, is the person who 'can do it twice'. Or, at least, keep on doing it . . .

But that is not quite the same as brainless routine. The digital habit frustrates creativity. So far from liberating us, Spotify customers repeat the same short playlist and are reluctant to explore the nearly infinite possibilities of their medium. And as if to confirm how the silicon culture of keypads and screens thwarts creativity, Adobe gives employees boxes containing coffee, chocolate, a paper notebook, pens and pencils. At a recent Silicon Valley conference, everyone had

a smartphone. But everyone had a Moleskine notebook as well. Just when paper was meant to be dead, Moleskine recently floated for $490 million, or approximately one Leonardo.

Digital culture tends towards standardised experiences, as if all perceptions and experience can be described by and contained in software. One day, someone will write creative code. But for the time being, creativity cannot be codified.

Artists versus the Establishment

▶ **Artists and writers comment end-lessly about the beauty of the world around them. Monet's exquisite paintings of his garden at Giverny and Wordsworth's sonnet 'Composed upon Westminster Bridge' would be two fine examples.**

But creative minds can criticise as well as admire: they don't just comment eloquently on what they like, they comment with equal eloquence on what they don't like. Their most frequent target is the world of politics and power. In both art and letters there is a long and honourable history of criticism of those who govern.

In the eighteenth century, James Gilray's cartoons satirised the mores and the leaders of his time with merciless accuracy, while Alexander Pope was doing the same in verse. In more recent times, Aldous Huxley's brilliant satire *Brave New World* exposed the dystopia to which he thought we were all headed. Soon after, George Orwell published *Animal Farm*, a stunning satire on communism, which he quickly followed with *1984*, a disturbing echo of Huxley's fears for our future.

In 1937, at the height of the Spanish Civil War, Picasso painted *Guernica*, a giant and emotionally charged canvas of despair and suffering. The town of Guernica, a bastion of the resistance movement, was bombed to destruction on behalf of Franco's nationalists. With cynical cruelty, Franco subcontracted the bombing to Hitler's

Guernica, **Picasso's tragic masterpiece**

air force. As the men of Guernica were away fighting in the war, the huge death toll was largely made up of women and children.

Picasso's profoundly disturbing painting became famous across the world as a vivid exposé of the horrors of war.

It is not surprising that creative minds use their craft to attack the political establishment. The very essence of creativity is the desire to find new paths, to express ideas in different ways, to question established thinking, to challenge the existing order.

And what are our political masters, if not the existing order? They are the embodiment of the status quo. Those who have power seek to keep it: so power resists change, and does so ferociously.

Through the centuries, artists and writers have questioned and opposed the established order. We should be grateful that those who inspire us are willing to challenge those who control us.

But we should not be over-confident about the potency of the creative world to hold power to account. This is a two-way street, and the established order always fights its corner with obsessive vigour.

Students of Stalin or of Hitler, indeed of any tyrant, will see a pernicious passion to control not just the media but every source of information, to protect their position and their power base.

It has ever been thus, and don't imagine it's getting any better. In Turkey, for example, the last few years have seen the despot Recep Erdogan turn his country from a model of secular democracy into a theocratic dictatorship. Question: What did dictator Erdogan do to achieve this? Answer: He stifled the press and he imprisoned the intellectuals. He knew that his battle for absolute power would not be fought with weapons but with ideas. Once the idea generators were behind bars, his tyranny was assured.

Another current leader with despotic leanings is Donald Trump, whose preoccupation with the media can only be considered paranoia. Endlessly railing against 'fake news' (which really means news that he doesn't want us to hear), Trump demonstrates the politician's desire to keep painful truths under the carpet. Sadly, in his case, this manipulation is expressed in a particularly exaggerated form.

Aeschylus said truth is the first casualty of war, and this remark is equally valid in a despotism, which is really a kind of civil war in disguise.

At a more modest level, we see our own Prince Charles use his power to suppress any creativity of which he disapproves – particularly in the field of architecture. Recently he leant on his friends in the Qatari royal family to stop a Qatari-funded residential development in Chelsea by the gifted architect Richard Rodgers. Some years earlier, he used his influence to stop an original and creative design by Ahrends, Burton and Koralek for a major extension to the National Gallery. The building that took its place is so anodyne in character that most Londoners who walk past it regularly still can't remember what it looks like. (Be honest: can you?)

With unparalleled irony, Charles made the speech that undermined the Ahrends design in 1984: the very same year in which George Orwell's novel of that name described a hideous world of universal government surveillance and repressive control of the individual. Nice timing, Charles.

Would you make it as an assassin?

▶ **Imagine you'd been hired to assassinate a president. You're only going to have one brief opportunity, at a public gathering, where he's going to be surrounded by a lot of other people. What would be your weapon of choice: a machine gun or a rifle?**

You're obviously going to choose the rifle – it just needs one accurate shot and the job is done. Choose the machine gun, spraying bullets around indiscriminately, and the likelihood is that you'll kill several of the wrong people but miss the right one.

This is an accurate, albeit rather morbid, metaphor for how people think about creativity. It's often assumed that if you rush out with dozens of ideas (the machine-gun solution), one of them will hit the target. For example, won't a professional photographer – armed with a modern digital camera – take hundreds of shots in the hope that one turns out the way he wants? Surely an advertising agency, pitching to a new client, will produce a sheaf of different approaches, expecting the customer to like at least one?

But in reality, exactly the opposite is true. One problem, however intractable, only needs one solution. But it must be the right solution. So the shrewd creative mind will concentrate only on finding the one right answer. Looking at a multiplicity of different ideas serves to confuse, not clarify. All too often, quantity is the enemy of quality.

The best designers and ad people work on finding one remarkable creative route. If the client won't buy it, you can go back and try again, but always with the goal of finding one answer, not a dozen alternatives.

Of course, there are plenty of ad agencies, design companies, etc., who go the machine-gun route, offering a great range of answers. But usually none of those answers are right. The agencies that work that way are less confident, and often less talented, than the folk who take a single-minded approach.

There is a compelling reason why the pursuit of one answer works, and why looking at a raft of ideas is distracting and dangerous. It's analogous to the reason that committees never produce good creative ideas. In a committee, each individual is subconsciously expecting one of the others to find a solution – so nobody does. You need one individual whose adrenalin is fired by the knowledge that it is their responsibility to get to the answer, and no one else's. Similarly, if masses of ideas are produced, the likelihood is that each of them will attack the target from a different direction, but none will hit the bullseye. Ten mediocre ideas don't add up to one good one.

To find a creative solution with true depth and force, you need to focus ruthlessly on one answer: you need one 'yes', not several 'maybes'.

The machine gun produces an endless volley of near misses, but with the rifle you hit the target once and destroy it.

Why then is there this belief in what I call the 'machine-gun philosophy': the notion that if you produce lots of ideas the law of averages will dictate that a few will be good?

The answer is that people who are not themselves very creative tend to underestimate the sheer difficulty of generating a good creative idea. They only see the results of creative thinking – a witty TV commercial, a moving song – and they never see the work that goes on to make the idea possible. So they never appreciate the importance of raw talent in creativity. They believe that if anyone produced a multiplicity of ideas, at least one or two of them would be good. But it doesn't work like that.

To understand that better, let's go back to the 'law of averages' argument. If I played a chess grandmaster at chess, he would win. Every time. It wouldn't make any difference whether I played him once or a thousand times, he'd always win. If I took a bucket of a hundred balls to the golf driving range and hit them all as hard as I could, none of them would go as far as one decent shot by Rory McIlroy or Jordan Spieth. So the law of averages doesn't work where talent is involved. It applies fine to questions of chance, but it doesn't work with questions of ability.

With modern digital cameras the focus is done for you electronically, and so is the exposure. This means that it's just about impossible to take a bad photograph. But the fact that you can't take a bad one doesn't make it any more likely that you'll take a good one. Because a great photograph needs to be more than just in focus and correctly exposed: it needs to be fuelled by a strong underlying idea. Whereas focus and exposure are purely mechanical issues, an underlying idea is anything but mechanical. It's to do with having a particular personal insight, an ability to articulate a personal vision. It's to do with talent, not technology.

There's an algorithm in your Canon or Nikon which ensures that it's always correctly focused, that your shot always gets the right amount of light. But there's no algorithm which can make you think and feel like Henri Cartier-Bresson or David Bailey.

Today's technology makes it harder to be bad, but it doesn't make it easier to be good. Because to be good you need a vision, and you can't replicate that electronically.

The assassin knows that to hit his target he needs one perfect shot, not a spray of random misses. Similarly, the artist knows that he needs one great idea, not a multiplicity of second-rate ones.

Is creativity over-rated?

Creativity is always, perhaps lazily, assumed to be a good thing. Although 'creative accounting' hints at criminality. Perhaps only in such an evidence-based culture as book-keeping would the presence of an unruly creative spirit be considered a damaging handicap.

But, being essentially contrarian, the creative spirit insists on interrogating itself. And the first question is: are you absolutely sure, after all the foregoing, that creativity is to be encouraged?

Before the Enlightenment, creativity was not much valued. Only when man replaced God did it take its place at the top of the hierarchy of human affairs. We have ever since been busy usurping the gods, a role first essayed by Prometheus himself.

And there's a long history of creativity (and genius) being associated with madness. The source is Seneca: '*nullum magnum ingenium sine mixtura dementiae fuit*', which Dryden parsed as:

Great minds are sure to madness near allied, And thin partitions do their bounds divide.

Every account of his obnoxious behaviour tempts amateur diagnosticians to suggest Steve Jobs had Asperger's Syndrome.

Still, even if being creative has its personal perils, no one seeks to be creative to make things worse for others. The very idea contains fundamentally attractive notions of nurture, culture (in its broadest sense), evolution and improvement. In short, to be 'creative' is to engage in the most meaningful way with life itself. Has anyone ever found themselves thinking of saying, 'Jobs, you evil, sleazy, rotten creative bastard!'? Probably not.

But creative people are, besides contrarian, not consensual; independent, not collective; unusual, not obvious; surprising, not predictable; perverse, not biddable; interesting, not boring; and alluring rather than dismissive. So, socially and organisationally speaking, costs and benefits are quite well balanced.

Elyn Saks, a mental health lawyer from the University of Southern California, thinks 'creativity is just one part of something that is mostly bad.' I imagine she has in mind case histories of creative types who presented with advanced cases of toxic megalomania and caustic selfishness; people intent on disruption rather than settlement; changers, not accepters.

Creativity may assume high intelligence and unusual perceptions. But it also assumes disturbance and restlessness, an endless cycle. The Romantics believed that poetry was not a matter of the writer's invention but an external force, which took possession of an individual, not always beneficially. The poet was simply a conduit for forces larger and more wonderful than his own imagination. To be creative, you had to be possessed by that Divine Fury: madness. Perhaps golf would lead to a happier life. There is no such thing as creative golf. But you want to be creative? Consider this awful passage from Ecclesiastes in the King James version: 'How dieth the wise man? As the fool.'

Amol Rajan is the BBC's media editor. This is an imperial BBC which long since abandoned leadership in anything, let alone creativity, and is now overwhelmed by a terrible confluence of strict observation, political correctness and the vilest tabloid celebrity-based sensationalism.

Anyway, Rajan, exploiting the BBC's threadbare authority, says: 'Wisdom begins with the realisation that original ideas are overrated.' This is a very creative insight. But I think it's wrong.

There is no ending:

creativity doesn't recognise boundaries

Can a kipper be creative?

▶ **When we speak about creativity, we tend to think first about the arts. Painting or composing music, for example, are obviously creative acts. The technologically driven media of today, such as TV, advertising commercials and films, are currently arenas of intense creative activity. Before you say that they are also arenas where the quantity is much more noticeable than the quality, I will agree with you – though there are some fine jewels in the dross. But they are creative activities, nonetheless.**

But it's narrow-minded to assume that these are the only places we can find creativity. The human imagination can apply its creative gift to all kinds of challenges. This is an issue we've explored in an earlier chapter, but it's of such fundamental importance to the role of creativity in all our lives that I'd like to return to it briefly.

> **The human imagination can apply its creative gift to all kinds of challenges.**

Consider, for instance, the problem for earlier civilisations, millennia before the invention of refrigeration, of how to preserve food. Someone, somewhere, experimented with the idea of suspending fish in hot smoke. This surely seemed a very odd thing to do at the time. But it worked: smoked fish last, and fresh fish do not, so this was a breakthrough in man's ability to survive the winter. It was also a breakthrough in flavour: the idea gave us such delicacies as smoked salmon and gravadlax, not forgetting the kipper, in my view the king of breakfasts.

If you look at a bicycle in the abstract, it seems an absurd concept: how could one possibly travel safely on something which appears so inherently unstable? It's amazing that anyone ever bothered to build one, since it's clearly going to fall over as soon as you look at it. Yet someone persevered with the idea, and now the bicycle is not only the most popular form of transport in the third world, it is, even in our high-tech age, the fastest-growing form of transport in the developed world.

The worlds of engineering and architecture are filled with instances of creative thinking. Consider the arch. Pillars supporting a roof need to be very close together if the roof is not to collapse between them. That's why the pillars round the Parthenon are so numerous. But the invention of the arch changed that. The weight above the arch is distributed downwards into the structure, so a great weight actually reinforces the arch rather than weakens it. It's a brilliantly creative concept.

Look at your own desk and you can see much humbler, but still very useful, examples of imaginative thinking. The modest paper clip is an unsung hero of office life. And the Post-it note famously came into being because an inventor found the glue he was using wasn't strong enough – which turned his curious mind to ponder what you could do with a glue that sticks, but not very well.

All of these ideas were born because someone made an imaginative leap and created a connection that had not been made before. Usually ideas evolve: they grow logically from what has gone before.

But sometimes evolution is displaced by revolution: there is an idea which doesn't follow on in an orderly way but stands previous thinking on its head. That's what I mean by 'an imaginative leap', and that is at the very heart of creativity.

So the roof of the Sistine Chapel is certainly highly creative, as is the *Mona Lisa*, the plays of Shakespeare or the music of Mozart. But – as we've seen – you can find creative thinking in much more mundane places.

So every time you use a Post-it note or breakfast on a kipper, remind yourself you are in touch with a genuinely creative thought.

There is no conclusion. There will never be

The creative thing would be to stop here and let you, the reader, get on with it.

Or include a page break and see what happens next.

The Cold War might be defined as that era between the Berlin Airlift and the Berlin *Mauerfall*, the one going up, the other coming down. It was the hangover from the Second World War, but recovery came fast.

For the West, prosperity was generous and seemed unlimited. There were paid holidays, pop music, television, consumer indulgence, sexual revolutions, jet travel. In France you had the *soixante-huitards* in miniskirts throwing cobblestones at gendarmes. Here we had women's liberation, moon landings, gay liberation, eventually even communists' liberation and other hitherto all but unimaginable freedoms.

In terms of creative freedom, a 1959 Cold War Cadillac in hot pink surely presents an argument that, in any culture, building such an opulent, ridiculous, frivolous spectacle of anti-environmental excess . . . meant anything at all was possible. Indeed, it was. So, in the same year, we got the Mini, the leanest and cleverest car ever. This was not what Oswald Spengler predicted in his miserably prophetic *Untergang des Abendlandes* (1922), it was the West's spectacular success. Three years after the Mini, the Beatles reached number one.

Yet it was also a period of great international anxiety. Just as today prosperous people like to build home cinemas in their basements, half a century ago they built bunkers to shelter from a nuclear attack that was always said to be imminent. In 1963, the US Army Corps of

Engineers identified 17,448 'fallout' shelters in New York alone, basements mostly, capable of housing over eleven million people. Their distinctive yellow signs, faded somewhat, can still be seen attached to buildings all over the city.

However, in retrospect, we can now see that the enormous military expenditure of a triumphalist US was the reckless sponsorship by insanely ambitious generals of technology that did not work with money that did not exist to smack down a threat that was never actually there. (Although it did give us some fabulous machinery as well as microwave ovens and Teflon, two unanticipated benefits of radar and space travel.)

The spectre of Soviet tanks advancing on, say, Sartre's Paris and interrupting his monologues over *apéros* at Café Flore was a propagandist's delusion. Those chugging and puffing Soviet T-54 diesels were so unreliable they could not be expected to travel a hundred kilometres from the Polish border without breaking down in a miasma of black smoke, at which point they would be nuked by B52s flying out of Mildenhall, Suffolk. And Soviet ICBMs would never have made it across the Atlantic . . . which is why President Kennedy became so alarmed when they were discovered only ninety miles away in Cuba.

But so extreme was the threat from the USSR deemed to be that the USAF and the Office of Naval Research funded extensive studies into creativity throughout the Cold War era. This was announced by J. P. Guilford in his 1950 address to the American Psychological Association. Read this now and the tone seems stilted, Dr-Strangelove-crazy, the message perhaps even more so.

Guilford, a prominent psychologist and a leader in intelligence testing (who firmly believed that the intellect could be defined by forty-seven factors), argued for research into creativity so better weapons could be designed. Only a torrent of new ideas would provide the United States with new weapons systems that were unimaginable to Pentagon dullards and pedestrian generals working in procurement. Surely there was something more exciting than Oppenheimer's bomb, described near the beginning of this book?

But Guilford touched on something else as relevant today as it was nearly seventy years ago. Hence, *How to Steal Fire*. Guilford was becoming aware that increasing industrial automation in factories was making factory work unsatisfying, marginalising human beings and favouring three-axis numerically controlled lathes. A new generation of intelligent machine tools made skilled workers redundant. They needed . . . creative stimulus so their potential might be realised elsewhere.

And now we have robotics and Artificial Intelligence. True, the threat from the East has changed from nostalgic Soviet missiles that were never launched and Warsaw Pact invasions that never came to daily invasions of container ships carrying Chinese consumer goods, but the prospect of robotics and AI now threatens at least as much destabilisation as thermonuclear war once did. Robotics, they say, will finally make manual work a thing of the past while Artificial Intelligence will bring redundancy and irrelevance to the professional, lettered classes as surely as the assembly line once brought redundancy and irrelevance to craftsmen. Your doctor, lawyer, architect and accountant will soon be replaced by apps.

What to do with sixty million redundant people crowded on to a cold island with few natural resources, a voodoo economy and misfiring institutions is a question beyond the scope of this book. But thinking creatively might, surely, be of some use or benefit to the newly unemployed. The creative thinker, the stealer of fire, when faced with a proposition, redundancy included, will consider it, then likely reject it because he will, or will soon, get a better idea. We cannot yet say what because it's in the nature of creative thinking that you never can: if it's predictable, it's not interesting.

Creative thinkers enjoy – and exploit – fluency of thought. They ignore fixed patterns. Prospects are unlimited because horizons do not exist. If you feel the same, I will feel different. Nor are there any boxes to think inside. It's not a matter of writing a symphony or a poem, although many may still wish to do so. But a symphonist and a poet have given us unmatchable insights into the creative mentality.

> **Creative thinkers enjoy – and exploit – fluency of thought. They ignore fixed patterns.**

Mozart composed entire symphonies in his head during uncomfortable carriage journeys between Vienna and Prague while at the same time fretting about his marriage and his money and the ever-present possibility of long-term unemployment. His mind became a kingdom, which he ruled with authority and the very greatest style. Discomfort and adversity were, in Mozart's case, no deterrents to the creation of divine beauty.

No one would deny that the poet Stephen Spender was a lesser artist than Mozart, but in 1946 he wrote an astonishing account of the business (for that is what it is) of writing. After the agonies of composition, the deferments, the hangovers, the midnight oil, the accomplished feeling of having written something well gave him 'intense physical excitement, a sense of release and ecstasy'. And who would not want to share such an experience?

Spender continued by explaining that in every other part of social or work life, you dealt with men, while 'In poetry, one is wrestling with a god'. Of course, conditions of working life have changed since

1946 and it is entirely possible to lead a busy working life in the company of machines alone.

But the presence of a god remains. And remains omnipresent in any discussion of creativity: in 1436 the great Florentine architect and theoretician of art, Alberti, wrote in *Della Pittura*, his treatise on painting, that artists may well consider themselves invested with divine powers. This idea is as old as Plato and has been recurrent ever since.

But *How to Steal Fire* began, as, indeed, did the world, with something even earlier: Genesis and the Christian God's defining Act of Creation. There followed Shiva and Prometheus. With creativity, you are always keeping company with the gods. And this is fine company if you want to avoid any feeling of oppression, impotency or uselessness.

Apart from that, there is no conclusion. There never can be. Creative thinking never stops Never even has a full stop

Prometheus Carrying Fire, Jan Cossiers

Acknowledgements

There's a reflex tradition in publishing that blame for a book should be equally shared between those who wrote it and those who made it possible. And that's only fair. Grateful authors know very well that their contribution is only a part of a larger and much more mysterious activity.

So you tend to find cringe-making and dutiful lists of all involved: visionary mother, long-suffering partner, tolerant wife, adorable children, generous editor, skilled typesetter, reliable courier, diligent library staff, inspired picture researcher, very inspired designer, Uber, fastidious printer, energetic bookseller, Majestic Wine, scrupulous accountant, friends too numerous to mention and loving pets (if appropriate). And of course, inclusive lists have the great advantage of disarming potential critics by inculpating them with the project's origins.

But shouldn't a book on creativity attempt a different sort of acknowledgements? And if yes, these would be a sort of confession. There's no bibliography here because if any books were consulted they are mentioned in the text. Instead, *How to Steal Fire* is a glorious memory dump: an edited, typeset and designed frame containing a lifetime's collection of anecdotes, observations, theories, suspicions, opinions, prejudices. Truth doesn't come into it. Why? Because a 'creative' view of the world is a matter of belief. And if that connects creativity to religion, a point is made.

That said, personally, three books discovered when I was very young remain inspirational models. Not just for *How to Steal Fire*, but for the conduct of life itself. Laszlo Moholy-Nagy *Vision in Motion* (1947) was the first book I read that convinced me everything is connected. Charles Biederman *Art as the Evolution of Visual Knowledge* (1948) was given to me by a kindly tutor. He said, 'You'll enjoy this,' and he was right. Then, the 1967 Penguin *The Medium is the Massage*, a brilliantly designed repackaging of Marshall McLuhan's memorable trope 'the medium is the message' from his book *Understanding Media* (1964).

Anyway, the result is this book. If it helps any reader in any situation say an emphatic 'Yes!' or even an emphatic 'No!', it will have worked. But returning to tradition in publishing, other culprits for whom serious thanks: Helena Gonda: editor. Claire Mason: designer. Catriona Hillerton: production. Charlie Brotherstone: agent. Yes!

Stephen is right. Author's acknowledgements usually sound tediously like those speeches by winners at the Oscars, where everyone bar the cleaning lady gets a mention. Even so, I do want to thank Charlie, and Helena, and the team around her. Without them, Stephen and I would still be sitting in a bar talking about it.

And I'd like to thank Stephen for putting up with me.

Finally, I'd like to thank me for putting up with him.

Picture
acknowledgements

David Bowie © Debi Doss/Getty

Mushroom cloud explosion © GL Archive/Alamy

The Anger of the Gods, 1960 (oil on canvas), René Magritte © Photothèque R. Magritte / Adagp Images, Paris, 2019. © ADAGP, Paris and DACS, London 2018.

Front cover of *The Medium is the Massage* by Marshall McLuhan, Quentin Fiore and Jerome Agel (Penguin Books, 1967). Copyright © Penguin Books, 1967.

Dejeuner sur l'Herbe, 1863 (oil on canvas), Manet, Edouard (1832-83) / Musee d'Orsay, Paris, France / Bridgeman Images

Eames chair sketch © Brennan Letkeman

Model T-Ford © Granger Historical Picture Archive/Alamy

The Labour of Ideas © Cara Mills. Photographer: Greg Barratt

Petworth, Sussex, seat of the Earl of Egremont, 1810 (oil paint on canvas), Joseph Mallord William Turner, exhibited © Tate, London 2018

Snow Storm - Steam-boat off a Harbour's Mouth, 1842 (oil paint on canvas), Joseph Mallord William Turner, exhibited © Tate, London 2018

Portrait of Proust © Photo 12/Alamy

Les Amants, The Lovers, 1928 (oil on canvas), Magritte, Rene (1898-1967) / National Gallery of Australia, Canberra / Purchased 1990 / Bridgeman Images. © ADAGP, Paris and DACS, London 2018.

Lolita poster © Moviestore collection Ltd/Alamy

Viagra tablet © Wyman/Sygma via Getty Images

Early Leica camera © icona/Alamy

Laudanum label © B Christopher/Alamy

Napoli © John McConnell of Pentagram. Reproduced courtesy of McConnell Design

Studebaker Avanti © Bob D'Olivo/The Enthusiast Network/Getty Images

Lockheed SR-71 Blackbird © Keystone/Getty Images

Box diagram © Olesia Misty/ Shutterstock

Set of crayons © Jovica Varga/Alamy

Miles Davis © Berliner Studios/BEImages

Michelangelo © GL Archive/Alamy

Einstein © dpa picture alliance/Alamy

Brain © Custom Medical Stock Photo/Alamy

Moleskine © Alexander Mazurkevich/Shutterstock

Guernica, 1937 (oil on canvas), Picasso, Pablo (1881-1973) / Museo Nacional Centro de Arte Reina Sofia, Madrid, Spain / Bridgeman Images. © Succession Picasso/DACS, London 2018.

Paperclip © zebicho/Shutterstock

Prometheus carrying fire, 1637 (oil on canvas), Cossiers, Jan (1600-71) / Prado, Madrid, Spain / Bridgeman Images

Index

Page numbers in *italics* refer to illustrations

Stephen Bayley, by Roger

On the surface, Stephen Bayley radiates style: chiselled features, easy charm, a perfect suit, and a hint of expensive scent. If he'd been born in the Regency era he'd have been Beau Bayley, strolling down a Nash terrace with a silver-topped cane under his arm.

But don't be deceived: while Stephen may cultivate the manner of a dilettante, the real Stephen is a very different animal. He is astonishingly well read, and the depth of his knowledge about the worlds of art, design and architecture puts the rest of us to shame. He doesn't just read about culture, he writes about it – extensively. He has published no less than twenty-two books, all concerned with different aspects of style, design and culture. He worked in academe as an art historian for many years before he and Terence Conran united to found the Boilerhouse at the V&A, which evolved to become the Design Museum, where Stephen was the first Director and its driving force. So when he writes about creativity, he knows what he's talking about. And when he writes, he writes beautifully.

My writing style is a bit like a Land Rover – workmanlike, good on rough terrain, but unlikely to win a *concours d'élégance*. Stephen's style is more like a Lamborghini – sculpturally shaped, striking, powerful, yet elegant. But Stephen's prose isn't just about style, gracious though that may be.

His writing is full of surprising and provocative insights. There is one marvellous moment in this book where Stephen describes an encounter with a government official who seeks Stephen's advice on how to increase levels of creativity. 'Make it illegal' is Stephen's rejoinder – witty, but also original, and perhaps even true.

His writing is perceptive, but also provocative. He is brave enough to be iconoclastic and irreverent when the mood takes him (which is often) and he can be laugh-out-loud funny.

Our working method is simple: we meet, and talk at length about everything but the job in hand. During these sessions, Stephen has educated me to survive, before noon, on a diet of strong espresso or, if later, several glasses of Albariño.

Squeezing two egos into one book isn't easy, but he makes it seem so. In truth, if it hadn't been for Stephen's encouragement I'd never have become a writer. So thank you, Stephen.

Or should I call you 'Beau' now? I think I will – I rather like it.

Roger Mavity, by Stephen

There's really no debating the notion that Roger is very annoying. And this, of course, is exactly what makes him interesting. And very good company. I have known him for a very long time, but for even longer I had a vicarious fascination with the business of advertising, the richly dunged field where Rog was cultivated. Heineken? Volvo? He was there when these classics of pop-culture sellebrity were created.

The sun has set on adland. But a generation ago ad agencies still maintained the culture where 'creative' was a job description. Creativity was institutionalised . . . even if that was an absurd process because properly creative people can tolerate all manner of discomfort (poverty, cold attics, strange haircuts, severe intoxication, deaf ears, hostile audiences), but cannot tolerate . . . institutions. Or what we might call 'boxes'.

In his agency days, Rog was no such thing as 'creative', at least insofar as job descriptions go. Instead he was one of the sub-species of adland who policed the jungle where the wacko 'creatives' lived, with their whims and expense accounts, busily overspending unlimited budgets.

But it would be wrong to see Rog's presence as a 'suit' as anything other than creative in its own right. Genius is nothing without the power of execution. And Rog was, indeed is, the sort of person who knows exactly where results fall in the hierarchy of creative activity.

In this sense, if in no other that comes to mind, he is similar to Enzo Ferrari. Over the portal of the famous sports car factory in

Maranello is an inscription from Ferrari himself: *I am not an engineer. I am not a designer. I am an agitator of men.* And this particular agitator of men produced really quite exceptional results without ever having to pick up a pencil, bash metal or struggle with a parallel-action drawing board.

Roger is an agitator. As I know. Like the mechanism that creates helpful turbulence in a washing machine, Rog engages with the suds of thought. And during that engagement, great benefits may become apparent in the wash. Certainly he is not inhibited by the genteel accommodations of agreement. Rog is magnificently disinclined to agree with any proposition, especially mine. Perhaps 'argumentative' is a better word. But, then, I enjoy argument.

Rog and I agree on very little. Music, theatre, sailing, bridge, politics; these things have no interest for me. In fact, if I could, I would have them banned. On the other hand, Rog is a polished enthusiast of each.

Of course, these disagreements are productive. We have an idea. Then we disagree about it. Not sure here if I am the glib but tuneful McCartney or the clever, headbutting cynic who was Lennon. Or, at least, Lennon's invented persona.

Fact is, however, without Rog's interventions and management, I would, being the feckless creative type – impulsive, restless – never have written this book. And surely that proves something.

Exactly what it proves, we will decide later.